Filling The Empty
ROOM

Poetry from the Series. November 2009

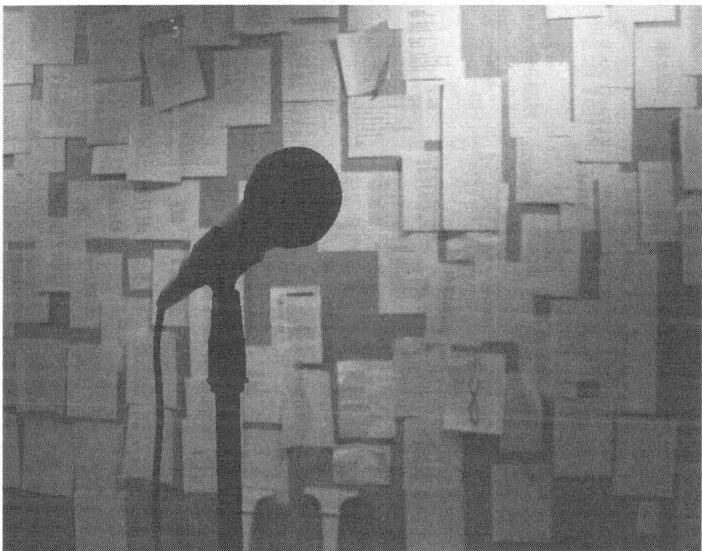

Edited by
Matt Mason

Filling The Empty Room: Poetry from the Series. November 2009

Cover design by JM Huscher

Publication of this book was generously supported by the Nebraska Writers Collective and the Seven Doctors Project.

Special thanks also to Doug Kiser and Peter Cales, Secret Penguin, Whatcheer, Rahul Gupta, Greg Kosmicki, The Backwaters Press, PoetryMenu.com, Sarah McKinstry-Brown, Katie F-S, Heidi Hermanson, and all local poets (those who read and those who didn't this time).

ISBN: 978-0-615-34738-7
First Printing: February, 2010

Published by:
Morpo Press
Matt Mason, Sovereign Editor
9712 N 34th St. • Omaha, NE 68112
mtmason@gmail.com

Printed in the USA by
Morris Publishing®
3212 E. Hwy 30 • Kearney, NE 68847
800-650-7888 • www.morrispublishing.com

EMPTY ROOM *BECOMES* ORGANISM
NOVEMBER 1st - 30th 2009

Contents

Washing the Body
Rebecca Anderson

I guess it's a nursing ritual. After all,
the mortuary will do it again,
more thoroughly. We stroke him
with warm cloths, soap-scented. We begin
at the hairline, work our way past places
mothers attend to: ears, neck, nose, elbows.
As I move down the trunk I debate
about the genitals. What would they think
if I touched him there? I recall
the morning when, craving comfort,
I picked the lock of my parents' bedroom door.
How he, erect, stalked out.
There's truth in this Electra business.
I'd thought myself a fitter partner
took his side in their rare squabbles
felt secretly superior. My mother,
undeceived, endured us both in silence.
The nurse in her knew how to heal.
Had she survived, he would still be here.
We wring our washcloths, lift his legs
ease on fresh pajamas, tuck the sheet
beneath his chin. I breathe his sweet hair,
hold my cheek to his brow. I wait for my
mother to enfold me.

Rebecca Anderson is an associate professor in the UNMC College
of Public Health. She teaches law and ethics at the University of
Nebraska Medical Center where she chairs the Ethics Consultation
Service.

Sonnet to the Radiologist (During an MRI)
Lindsey Anne Baker

I used to think love looked like this: his house,
us both in different rooms not speaking; alone
in bed at morning I could hear him spoon
the coffee—He'd bring me toast. We'd read the news.
You're in a different room and I pretend
the sound I hear is a knife scraping a dish
and I'm lying down after breakfast, a little sick.
You enter, take my hand, ask after my head.

I close my eyes, envision his eyes for yours,
his mouth instead above my own—So joined
in thought, the mind's recess you cannot see,
I can stand to live with you. If living's less
than what I dream, I'll still take flesh's shock,
the blind, brief touch, the near reality.

Lindsey Anne Baker is a poet and journalist in Omaha, Neb. Her poetry has appeared in the *Nebraska Review, Left Facing Bird, Hospital Drive* and *The Benefactor.*

Selection from the opening chapter of a completed book, Inscapes: Memoir of a Spiritual Journey
by Bette-B Bauer

In the early 1980s, I worked at a small hotel on Jost Van Dyke, a tiny island in the British Virgin Islands. The only access to the island was by boat, and we either walked or took a dingy between the three small harbors. It was paradise – 80 degrees everyday, trade winds keeping us cool.

Huge schools of baitfish would often appear in the bay. Their small, silvery bodies would coalesce into large, circling forms, turning from dark to vivid silver as they swirled back and forth in the protected lagoon, tossing the sunlight off their pirouetting bodies. One day I decided to explore their world, and swam slowly into the midst of one of these schools, trying to contain my fear of being nibbled. In the middle of the school, I could see nothing except the dancing forms of baitfish all around me, refracting the sunlight as I floated with them, and with the undulations of the ocean. All that I could hear beneath the water was the beat of my heart, and the distant thump of waves hitting the beach.

Suddenly, the baitfish sprayed out in all directions, opening up the space directly in front of me to reveal a huge sea turtle, less than a foot from my face. We were both suspended together in that moment, one of the turtle's wild eyes turned to my masked face, and then we simultaneously began to back away madly from this meeting. The turtle then turned, and swiftly disappeared into the azure distance, leaving the water around me empty.

This memory calls to my imagination frequently, no matter what I am doing – bundling up in down clothing against a snowy day, sitting in the whirlpool at the YWCA, suffering through the abstract rhetoric of a meeting, or walking out of the middle of a seminar to follow the sounds of a marimba.

Bette-B Bauer: after careers as a jewelry designer, cook, and accountant, Bauer is now an Associate Professor of English at the College of Saint Mary in Omaha, Nebraska. Her area of research is Women's Spiritual Journeys in Literature, and she has just completed a memoir entitled *Inscapes: Memoir of a Spiritual Journey.*

Jack Goes to Town
by JV Brummels

He stands bare-bellied in his drawers
in a door that cuts motel-room dark
from the milk-white light before sunrise
watching the red-haired girl with nightmares
drive her hail-dented Ford off the lot

His boots stand upright like a suggestion
but he winds himself back into rumpled bedding
until he's breathed all perfume from the pillows

He rises dresses sets his hat on his head
walks back streets to the doughnut shop
for the early-bird special
The sun climbs up over the hill of earth
and night's gone

Square shadows of 19th century storefronts
race away to the west
Something to get up for Jack thinks
these cutouts of black against first light on brick
the best view of a dead architecture

He strolls past the blank stares of plate glass
licking sugar glaze from his fingers
On a morning without wind
frayed yellow ribbons and battered flags
hang like men from light poles

He finds his car in front of the south-end bar
turns the key
Bells and whistles arrayed on the dash
the only morning action on Main

Rapists insist
young men persist

but on a sunny morning
Jack cruises along all the miles home
seeing forever from the tops of hills
whistling
even with no end to war in sight

J V Brummels' collections include *Book of Grass* (2008 Nebraska Book Award for Poetry), *Cheyenne Line and Other Poems, Sunday's Child, 614 Pearl* and 2009's *City at War.* His work has also been recognized with a National Endowment for the Arts Literature Fellowship, the Elkhorn Prize and the Mildred Bennett Award for contributions to the state's literature from the Nebraska Center for the Book. Rancher and longtime professor at Wayne State College, where he coordinates the Plains Writers Series and the Downtown Slam, he's also published short fiction and a novel. In his spare time he publishes Logan House.

Stairways
by Michael Catherwood

You are lost, forget the number of steps
down the dark stairway. Your hand guides you
along the cold plaster walls. Your brother

breathes under the covers and you hear
his chest wheeze under the dusty curtains.
A sliver of daylight pierces the shadows.

See, everything returns, begins again
as if lives never ended, lives thirsty
with promise. Oh, we are all lost then found

in those familiar passageways
that reappear and resurrect in all
those friendly stairway penumbras.

Michael Catherwood lives and writes from Omaha and his book
Dare is published by The Backwaters Press. He has been reader
and essayist for *Plainsongs* for over 13 years.

Paranoia
by Devel Crisp

When looking upon this piece,
You may think that you are reading these words
When actually,
These words are reading you!

Analyzing every reaction and thought you may carry while you
harmlessly skim
over them.

Not true, you may think?
Well look them dead in their "i's" and tell them that!

Yeah, sure,
Someone thought of these words to write,
But that only because the words allowed him to.

And while you e reading for relaxation,
They think it a staring contest,
And you lose every time.
Sorry.

They truly thank you for reading them, though.
They e tired of being cooped up on this stiff, dry paper.
So they run a muck in your brain,
And press a lot of buttons.

These little suckers are very feisty and opinionated, aren they?

But remember
Anything that has an opinion-
can rebel.

Good day.

Oh, and by the way,
The title of this piece finds you extremely attractive.

A unique, innovative voice, spoken word artist, Devel Crisp has been captivating listeners from his hometown of Omaha, Nebraska for a few years. His aim is to inspire, engage and entertain audiences with his creative creations.

On Her Second Birthday
by Cat Dixon

I'm eating, eating, eating her hair –
stringy, fine baby hair and I'm waiting,
waiting for the reverse of birth –
take her in again, quiet the tantrums.
Can the earth implode? Can volcanoes
suction up their magma once it has
become lava? Will the melted path
awaken – trees erect, skin return
to bone? When I laugh, she scratches
the back of my throat. When I rest,
I hear her groans.

Cat Dixon earned her MFA from the University of Nebraska and is now an adjunct instructor and a church office administrator. She is the volunteer Marketing Director for The Backwaters Press out of Omaha, Nebraska and a mother of two. Her work has appeared in *Eclectica, Sugarhouse Review, Poetryfish* and is forthcoming from *Coe Review.* catdix@gmail.com

So long as we posses our own
by Sara Lihz Dobel

I had never seen a hurricane but then it came to me, waves
of wind and water sweeping a picnic table,
and a statue of Mary, into my window. The glass
held, though I heard it creek and spit against the storm, as I
bunkered down in the bathroom, worried about the cat.

She had not seen a hurricane either, and both of us
out of our element, she was the brave one standing
sentinel, in my Nebraska window, watching all
the water. There is nothing
like a storm to pluck the fingers from the trees.

That summer the rain rivered its way though the low plains,
making bathtubs of basements, sweeping us all out to see
what kind of a land we had tried to tame.

When the lakes are full, the rivers cannot empty, so the sandbars
sprouted phragmites like tentacles, raising the islands, raising
the rivers, sending their cargo seeping in creaks and streams
through the firmly packed dirt of mainland.

They've been spraying the Platte River sandbars, killing
the trees, the weeds, the small lives hiding there. It was an
        accident.
They just meant to make room for the river,
they said. They were just
trying to give the water someplace to go. The water
will not flood next spring, but it will strip the bark
from the willows on the east bank. They will weep
further into the way. They will not make it to fall.

Sara Lihz Dobel received her MFA from California College of the Arts in 2007, and returned to Omaha where she has represented her city at all three national tournaments. She currently teaches English at Dana College and Metropolitan Community College.

"I like to think of myself as the official back-up go-to for Omaha poetry events, whether it's fundraising for the team, substitute hosting a slam or an open mic, reading an opening poem for a feature, facilitating workshops by out-of-town poets, or hosting them in my casa, I like to do a lot of little things to try and makes things run better."

PROUST STOPS IN FOR A DRINK AT DAN'S PLACE
by Eve Donlan

I

Wandering the side streets in search of Dan's Place, I picture
something out of Norman Rockwell: A slow turning ceiling fan, a
white and black linoleum floor, Hank Williams on the radio.
The stocky, short order cook (maybe it's Dan himself) takes your
order, spatula in hand, the anchor on his bicep showing beneath
the T shirt sleeve.
Perched on his head is one of those white paper caps with a
vaguely military look.
The cigar hanging out of one corner of his mouth gives him a
disreputable air, but boy can our guy cook.
He'll whip up a fried egg and onion sandwich while you drink your
coke at the lunch counter, and don't order the cheeseburger basket
unless you're really hungry, Mac.

II

But when I arrive, Dan's Place turns out to be a tiny, dark café,
where, at a table on the cobbled walk, you might find your
Proustian narrator drinking with his friend, le Monsieur Baron, not
focusing on the baron's complaints about the lesser nobility; but
instead remembering the contours of a room, a room in which he
can imagine himself if he slightly closes his eyes, a porch in the
evening on which, long ago, he sat with his eyes slightly closed,
listening to the clinking of silverware against plates and the
murmur of adult conversation, dreading the moment when he
would be sent upstairs to bed without hope of his mother coming
up to kiss him good night.

The Baron leaves with the woman in the pink dress.
I study the wrought iron menu-board.
The waiter (could this be Dan?) brings another cognac.
I watch our narrator out of the corner of one eye, recalling his
dream of visiting a certain town in France, a town he'd envisioned
full of crystal spires and bells because of the way its name rang out
in his imagination! but which, once he arrived, turned out to be an
ordinary seaside village. It was a shock to a sensitive fellow like
him, but after a few days he adjusted.
Looking around at Dan's Place, I understand just how he feels.
Confronted with the striped awning, the wooden shutters, I feel
displaced, like a character in book that nobody reads.
Ah, the power of suggestion: It's not that my imaginary diner was
better than yours, and so far no one's accused me of being the
sensitive type, but I was all set for a deluxe hamburger. Give me
another minute and I'll adjust to the idea of tea and madelines.

Eve Donlan is an adjunct instructor of English at UNO and a
board member of the Nebraska Writing Center Consortium. She is
probably STILL reading *Remembrance of Things Past*.

Poem of 4 Explanations to Poems at Poetry Readings

by Gary Dop

I
by one of those ladies
with the red hats and purple shirts

I just wanna say
about this piece
you need to know
that I own 30 cats
and that the river
near my house is called Clementine
and so is my Siamese,
who appears in this poem
as one of my hats.

II
by Doug, someone's roommate
until the body-shaving incident

This one is for a lady I called "mother"
in this poem, but my mother's here tonight,
Hi Mom, so we'll just say "Mother"
is a lady named Helga
but for the sake of the poem's integrity
we'll still say "Mother". Entitled
"I hate your face."

III
by the wide-eyed guy
nobody has ever seen before

Before I got out of prison
me and the guys in my cell
wrote a poem about dancing

that resonates with me
so if we could all stand together
and hold hands and think
of death row—I'll read
"The last dance of innocent Rico."

IV
by a lit. major named Shirley
with the dark black hair

This poem totally speaks
for itself so I don't need to tell you anything
except in book II of Paradise Lost
when Satan must move through
Hell's mouth he meets
his wife slash daughter Sin
and son slash Sin's lover, Death.
Oh, and the color red symbolizes blood.

Gary Dop grew up throughout Germany and the Midwest, received his MFA from the University of Nebraska, and now lives with his wife and three daughters in Minneapolis, where he directs the Taproot Reading Series and moonlights as a professor, playwright, and stand-up comic. Dop's poems have appeared recently in *New Letters, North American Review, Agni, Poet Lore, Rattle, Poetry Northwest,* and the *American Life in Poetry* newspaper column. Email: garydop@gmail.com / Website: www.garydop.com.

This poem was first published in *Rattle*.

FOR JASON
by Lorraine Duggin

> So soon I shall be gone—
> I'm but a morning glory,
> A fleeting face-at-dawn.
> Moritake (1472-1549)

I never see morning glories
without seeing your face,
sweet, shy smile of greeting,
bright, unexpected presence

that graced the earth
twenty-six years. You died
of poppies, accidental
overdose, your favorite
flower then, introduced
to you by your besotted papa.

But mine, morning glories,
unforgettable, the day
of your funeral, arriving back home.

They greeted me
first time that summer.
I had waited, waited for them
to open, and finally

on the saddest day, blossoms gushing
purple veins

moist eyes momentarily
blinded by the glare

my unexpected joy
at seeing them,
like seeing you.

They rested at the corner
of the house, bejeweled
network of petals in fluted,
full, funneling bloom,
clinging to twining
needle-thin vines,
the bursting deep purple
of broken vessels

vulnerable as a private whisper,
a promise, their early beauty
transient, delicate
as your bright smile
remembered, fragile as a life.

Lorraine Duggin lives in Omaha and teaches at Metropolitan
Community College, where she received an Excellence in Teaching
Award in March, 2009. She has a Ph.D. in English/Creative
Writing from UN-L and is a Master Artist with the Nebraska Arts
Council and Iowa Arts Council in the Poets in
Schools/Communities programs. Her writing has received
recognition with a Nebraska Arts Council Poetry Award, a
nomination for a Pushcart Prize, the Mari Sandoz Prairie Schooner
Short Story Award, a Maude Hammond Fling Dissertation
Fellowship, an Academy of American Poets' First Prize, among
others, and her poetry, fiction, and non-fiction have been
published in many periodicals, anthologies, textbooks, and
newspapers. She can be reached by writing to
lduggin@mccneb.edu.

Kansas
by Andrew Ek

The best thing about Northwest Kansas is the stars.
The nearest stop-light is 25 miles away
in the absence of artificial light
I have a full view of the cosmos,
I know what infinity looks like.

The stars remind me of when I was
eight years old, and my father and I stood
out in the backyard finding constellations.
My favourite was Orion, the hunter.

It's been several years since I last used my
star-map, but at night, when I go driving,
I look for the Hunter's belt.
It is something familiar.

I teach children. I teach them English.
I thought this meant reading and writing
and talking about life.

Instead, it means sentence diagrams,
seating charts and worksheets,
how to get through the weight of the day,
but mostly how to shut up and take it
I am learning patience.

My students are farmers;
they grow crops
they skip my class to go hunting when
the weather's right.

On the fourth day of school, Tyler
asks me if I would go to church with him.
I lie.

I do not tell him that I don't believe in the things I can't see,
or that I spend most of my time wanting to escape to somewhere
      better.

I do not tell him that I am disappointed in how small
I've become lately, how limited I am these days, and
I sincerely hope that this isn't the size I've been all along,
but that I've just shrunk for a while.
I've forgotten what infinity looks like.

I don't tell him about how I take a long hot shower
every morning to release the muscles in my back
so that I can sit comfortably.
By the time I get out, the mirror is
so fogged up that I can't see myself at all.
I don't believe in the things I can't see.
It's the only way I get through the day

And I forget sometimes what a better place looks like,
so I feel less inclined to try to run.
Some days, I can't tell if my feet are sinking,
or if they're just sprouting roots.

Still, most days are good, and I am happy
when I am at the front of the room, even though
I usually wake up shouting "Motherfucker" at my ceiling.
I am learning to keep my mouth shut.

We are reading TS Eliot when Jace interrupts me and
asks if this is all there is, if life ever gets better after high school,
because if it doesn't, he might as well give up now
because he has seen and done everything.

I tell him that I think it does, and that the world
is not small forever. I don't believe in the things
I can't see, and I have forgotten how to see myself
but I still believe in this, and even if I do not belong here,
and even if I cannot see it, I still believe in home.

And yes, most days are good, but at night when
I want to escape I go driving on the highway west of town
which has no stoplights or street lights and I pull off to the side
in the middle of darkness and stare up at the stars so I can
      remember
what infinity looks like, because I've forgotten.

and for a minute I'm eight years old again in the backyard with my
      father,
and we are looking for Orion. I am learning about infinity.

I am learning to look for it even when I can't see it

I am learning how my feet grow roots
even when I feel I am sinking and out of place

I am learning what a better place looks like,
one I won't want to escape.

I am learning about home.

Andrew Ek is a teacher and writer who calls Lincoln his home. He
has been a member of two slam poetry teams (both from Lincoln)
and is a regular at both the Lincoln and Omaha slams. He is one of
the owners of The Apollon, an arts and entertainment hub set to
open in late 2010. Andrew is also on the board of directors for the
Nebraska Writers Collective (run by Matt Mason), and spends
much of his time researching, discussing and writing about
education reform, and also playing tennis.

Mother Death
by Deirdre Evans

Pushing a cart through Wally World mart
I'm staring at panty hose and paperbacks and gift wrap paper
when this newspaper headline slams into my head:
YOUR MOTHER IS DEAD. YOUR MOTHER IS DEAD.
Why just a month ago I trolled these same isles
hunting down adult protection: what would work best for an aging
       leaky mommy
who begs not to wear a diaper,
no not that indignity, though the bed stinks, the carpet stinks, the
       bathroom
and the house and the wheelchair stinks.

Over now. Done with.
No more dilemmas of dignity. No mother left at all.
Although some lady is lying in her casket. I touch her artfully
       clasped hands and she is cold.
She is cold.
As if I were the first daughter to loose her mother.
My mother's mother died. And her mother, too. At age 42 from
       consumption.
And she gave away her 2-year old daughter to a childless Civil War
       widow aunt, and cried and cried because she knew she
       would never see that child again.

Always and *never* and *forever* are stupid words for us to even learn.
As if such concepts could have any truck with folks of flesh and
       bone and blood and guts.
Fuck with us is more like it.
The thing with dead people is that they stay dead.
My mother has remained dead for over a year.
Driving to the cemetery last spring , we passed by a ranch house
       with a garage sale
sprawled across the driveway, and I wanted to tell the drive to
       stop!, so we could check it out.
Since there could be no hurry now (and maybe we would find a

bargain).

Later I stood apart, looking down the row of graves, trying to
      memorize this death party: the clusters of grand children,
      the curve of the road, a tree next to the canopy,
my father in a wheelchair, staring at his knees.
Yet even two days later my sister and I could not find the grave.
We wandered urgently, searching amongst the old carved angels
      and the newer glossy, laser-cut granite, before we found
      Mom's trash heap of roses--still there after all.
A nearby RV factory was now filling the spring air with a nasty
      plastic stench
and a grating, low pitched machinery whine.
Well, she wouldn't mind all that now, but it sure annoyed the hell
      out of me.

It will get better, everyone said it. And everyone was right.
When my mother began to visit my dreams, I awoke comforted.
Dream or not, the healing was real.
The jagged hurt washed smooth by sorrow, her memory resides in
      me now like a pearl.

Deirdre Evans is an aging hippie who ended up married and is
living happily ever after.

Pills
by Steven Evans

Listen up, my friends!! Got bursitis, arthritis, bunions or the flu;
    got cancer or ebola or malaria too?
Got bad breath or diarrhea or constipation so bad your face turns
    blue?
Well America's got the answer: there's a pill for you

Yes, there's a pill for the ladies if they sweat at night, or if there's
    cellulose where your ass was once tight.
Can't sleep or you're fat or just want your boobs looking so big you
    can't believe it's true,
or you're 2 months late and you're not sure just which boyfriend
    might have done it with you?
Don't worry your little head — there's a pill for you!

Now I found an ad the other day — said was I wasting time going
    to pray
why waste the time it said — no burden to carry
 — why, every one of their little pills was worth 10 Hail Mary's.

There was a yellow one for simple venal sins which got my
    attention
and there were blue ones for mortal sins -- it said use with
    discretion
Well I couldn't remember what I done Saturday night, it's true —
so I popped 3 yellow ones and a hand-full of blue.

On Sunday, I saw Father O' Riley without a hint of remorse.
He asked me how long it had been since my last confession, of
    course.
I said, "Father — it doesn't matter now — I took 5 of these pills
    each worth 10 Hail Mary's
Lucky Walgreens was open and those pills they now carry."
Well, he was not amused and said "My son, in the Church we must
    trust,
so from here on in, you better buy those pills from us!

— 'cause ours are approved by Jesus, Joseph, and Mary — as well
        as the Trinity
or your soul will go straight to hell — on that you can trust me."

But then I saw an ad that said they had just what *I* needed
— would make my manhood enlarged and I would be greeted
by any woman with a sigh and a smile; would improve my
        performance by a country mile.
Each bottle promised to add a full inch so I bought a dozen — no
        big deal.
Figured if that caused any problems, I'd just buy shoes with a very
        high heel!

But there *w as* a small problem which I noticed in the fine print.
I may have to stop taking those pills — this was my hint:
The insert said "Discontinue if you constantly barf,
            – suddenly develop an uncontrollable cough,
                – or check with your doctor if your penis falls off."

Du'oh !!! On second thought maybe I can just stay healthy —
        which would be quite dandy.
Stop eating so much, exercise, and cut out the candy
"Waiter I think I'll just have a side of broccoli with my seaweed
        order,
and also bring me a tall glass of purified water ...
... 'cause I gotta take my pills !'"

Steven Evans has been a NASA rocket scientist, on the faculty of schools of engineering and business, and a research scientist in health care systems, genetic sciences, nursing informatics, hereditary cancer, cancer therapeutics and nutraceutical science. He is currently writing a second book using quantum physics to explicate Kabbalah — and hopes to soon figure out what he wants to do when he grows up.

HAIKU TO FILL THE VACANCIES
by Katie F-S

Release the sparrow
wrapped in your ribs. He will steal
away with your tears.

THE FAT CAMP VALEDICTORIAN'S ONLY POSTCARD HOME
by Katie F-S

Last night I licked
my nipples and wished
upon the whipped
cream moon for a rocketship
planted in your backyard,
my eleven o'clock astronaut,
and a landing pad
the exact right size
centered smack
dab flat on my
mattress.

Katie F-S has posed as many things in her many lives, including poet, playwright, preschool teacher, muppet, and person who needs glasses to see. She is generally overcaffeinated and has more tattoos than her mother knows about. She has a scar on her chin from proving she can fly. Furthermore, she plans to now speak exclusively in the third person; it's the most fun she's had all day.

∞

by Dominique Garay

I am aware of the fact
that I am aware
that I can see
that I have this body
and that I can create an effect
I can communicate
I can have my own thoughts and ideas
independent of anyone else

I see these things and I realize
that I am the creator and the cause point of what troubles me
that I allow myself to fall
that I must take some responsibility for what was done to me
by others, by myself
and what I have done to others
and what others have done to others

maybe that's too much
but I should do something
even if it's just looking upon these acts
and frowning upon them, speaking out against them
I can set an example in the way I live
in how I treat others
and how I experience what life throws at me

I want to love
in spite of
every invitation
not to

I want to be sane about this
I want to be free
I want to defend myself and others
and I want to live

I want to live life as it was meant to be

Just a few square feet

If I were to tell you
where I have been
it would be too graphic

and it makes me feel good
that you even care
that you're presenting yourself in front of me to listen
I kind of feel like I already told you everything
that's how kind you look
that's how comfortable you make me
I wish I could buy a few lots of the space that surrounds you

Dominique is an inspirational poet and electrifying performer. He
has been performing and conducting creative writing and
performance workshops since 2000. His poetry is for everyone, as
it address areas in life that are real to people. In 2005, Dominique
had the honor of sharing the stage with Ted Kooser (Poet Laureate
and Pulitzer Prize Winner for Poetry) in an NETV special.
Dominique represented Nebraska at the National Poetry Slam in
both 2003 and 2006 as a member of the Omaha Poetry Slam
Team. In 2006 Amnesty International named Dominique a "Poet
of Conscious". Currently, he is working on a children's book with
an accompanying DVD.

In November
by Shelly Clark Geiser

My father died,
my grandmother died,
my sweet Calleen died,
my loyal dog died,
my aunt,(the one who loved me best), died
in November.

That's why I get a little nervous
as the October days tick away.
But, almost imperceptibly, November arrives.

So, I go outside,
look up and into the cloudless sky,
a giant bowl of blue
full of memory and story.
It is so quiet out here
except for a few leaves crunching under my feet
and the far off screech of a hawk.

There's not much wind, save for a little breeze,
but it carries that whisper that needs no decipher:
Says, yes, winter is coming,
but not yet.
Says, today will be warm and full of great color,
but, a few minutes shorter.
Says pay attention,
be ready for the next thing.

For me, the next thing is
a grasshopper
who has now fixed itself to
the glass of the screen door.

Old Veteran of summer fields,
it is late, your camouflage is fading,

your blood runs green.
How far have your leaping legs taken you?
How many songs have you sung with your wings?

Even now, when I open the door
then close it,
you do not flinch.
I say, stay strong, you old codger,
it's November.

Shelly Clark Geiser coauthored with Margorie Saiser an anthology of Nebraska writers entitled, "Road Trip: Conversations with Writers," published by Backwaters Press and winner of two Nebraska Book Awards. Shelly's poems have been anthologized in "Times of Sorrow, Times of Grace" and "Nebraska Presence: an Anthology of Poetry". She lives in Omaha.

Out Loud
by Marissa Gill

Sliding door wombs
closed off
icy
broken
and once mine.
My fingers
dull knives
sharpened by my cheeks
tears rusting
and green coppered
leave me
punching
air absent of breath
and inconsistency.
This is where pain grows,
tulips
and daffodils,
brown grass
piercing my feet
bleeding
from my chest
thumping as I run
flat on my back
unable to rest
until she stops screaming
wordlessly
away from him
always away from him
like rivers and mountains;
I am wishing for lakes
and buoys.

Ring fingers
that are dull and unfettered
feel like gangrene

hot blood shedding it unto wrists
fragile like hers,
to shoulders like Atlas.
I am wrapped in a desert
of frozen I love yous
she can't breathe out long enough
to melt.
I am burning
and sleeping standing up
waiting for dragons
holding broken swords
throwing away shields
that never bore my family crest
anyway.

Please light candles for me,
light poems,
light mornings,
light forgiveness,

make it glow
so wise men will follow.

This is breaking
personified through skin
paint cracking on portraits of children
that sit still
eternally
like lips
taught silence
before mother.
I am drinking amniotic fluid
choking on infancy
and regurgitated empty boxes
of what I once called sustenance.

Smiling like lost children
I am leaving home

to save it as it burns,
stopping to stare at frames
holding memories like
waterfalls.
I am reflections,
a prism of indecision
and sharpened anger,
waiting to blind
my attackers before their intentions
can be deciphered
in the middle of the night
that longs for sun
like a lover
whose faults have all been forgotten.

The taste of salt
leaves me searching for gulls
hoping for feathers
found on wet rocks,
hoping I can still take flight
again someday,
knowing the sky is closer now
since I've lifted my head off the pillow.
Forget me like lyrics
of a song sung too many times,
and leave my melody
outside the window
so the breeze can catch it
and place me where I always belonged.

Sleep well
in leaves made of second guesses and
repressed memories
of what never came to be.

Sleep well,
and wake me
when the sun

finally
rises.

Marissa Gill is a singer/songwriter and poet from Omaha,
Nebraska. She has been doing slam for four years and was on the
Omaha Slam Team in 2006 and coached the 2007 Lincoln Slam
Team. She has one chapbook entitled *Born and Raised*.

Barger Street, Midnight
by Lauren Goldstein

Two black labs and Buford
the hound—hocks and knees
knobby, ribs straining under fur—

curl at Matt's feet as he strums
a Gibson electric, back turned
to a turquoise tapestry.

His band jams in front
of a projector screen,
the beat thrums, swirling

with purples and limes
of set lights strung
from the ceiling like torches.

Thick cables and tech wires,
duct taped to mechanical board
walls that insulate the apartment

snake behind the band's digital
digital backdrop. When the clock
rolls to 2 a.m., soundboards still flicker

red and green, tattooed hands cue
bass and treble, slide in sync
with guitar chords. The labs stir,

open an eye, wag tails as Tiny-2-Tone,
in a tie-dye Dead shirt scrapes
open the storm door, slings

his southern accent like an aphrodisiac.
The room passes back glances
and Rolling Rock while he picks up,

plucks for tune and eases the strings
to match Matt's groove. They lean back,
feel the buzz of notes, and wait

for nothing more than
the next change in key.

Lauren Goldstein resides in Midtown Omaha with her boyfriend, Tiny. You may recognize her as your neighbor who is in constant fury-filled pursuit of her escape artist dogs. She graduated from Virginia Tech in 2008 with her MFA in creative writing. She is currently a Resident Assistant Professor of English at Creighton University where she teaches Freshman Comp and World Lit and is at work on a second collection of poems.

An Answer for Everything
by Neil Harrison

On camera, on the radio,
I've heard them ranting on
and on about a failed economy
they long ago soared far above,
a war they have no personal stake in,
a religion founded on humble love
they've somehow warped into a means
to damn us all in that private hell
they preach, full of arrogance and hate.

These self-appointed pundits with
an answer for everything, nothing ever
out of reach of their egocentric
ramblings on this precarious planet,
where not one of us can be
sure of our next heartbeat,
another wholly unearned gift
pulsing forth from the mystery
that both surrounds and fills us.

And all at once clear
as the sudden dawn of insight,
that shining proverb comes to mind—
the more I learn, the less I know—
and I find myself then pitying
that dearth of education,
the hopeless depths of ignorance
in anyone with such a ready
answer to it all.

Neil Harrison's poems have been collected in *Story* (Logan House, 1995/96), *In a River of Wind* (Bridge Burner's, 2000), and *Into the River Canyon at Dusk* (Lone Willow, 2005), and his fourth collection, *Back in the Animal Kingdom,* is nearing completion. He teaches English and Creative Writing at Northeast Community College in Norfolk, Nebraska, where he runs the Visiting Writers Series.

When You Crashed The Ninja ZX6RR
by Carolyn Helmberger

Your second degree burn
was the shape of Ireland,
an island of devastation
in an alabaster ocean.
There were mountains of raised
black skin, rivers and valleys
where flesh was ground away.
Bloody tributaries flowed
to the surface trying
to heal this isle from
inside out. Foothills peeling,
an imprint of heat, pavement
and speed. When you called
from the E.R. you told me
your tires had skidded
out from under you,
but the bike was ok.

Carolyn Helmberger is a native of Omaha, Nebraska. In January 2008 she received an M.F.A. in creative writing from the University of Nebraska. She currently works at the University of Nebraska Medical Center in the Department of Neurological Sciences. She has been published in *The Pedestal Magazine, Language and Culture Review, Plainsongs,* the upcoming issue of *Free Lunch,* and others.

Memento Mori—Remember That You Are Mortal

by Heidi Hermanson

We are transients, our stint short,
nothing more than a twig
that randomly snaps in two, no more significant
than a stain from a wine glass
laid carelessly on yellow parchment.

We dawdle, as shadows darken,
gaslight reality,
shrug at time's larceny
as we loiter, gazing off into the distance,
deep in thought, preoccupied.
A lull.
      Here are the kids,
precious faces, serious, stoic,
obsidian eyes staring into the future.
In the background, some books,
some wine—everything you need, really.

The shroud of recollection
is a wistful veil, how time smudges
memory in a soft lens!
Under nocturne, rogue stars revealed,
--all sparkle and crushed glass--
and covered everything like a mantel. Even time.
.

But now our limbs tremble, we surrender and
abandon everything as the minute hand absconds with out bones
time varnishes our memories in warm sepia tones,
a lens we fall through willy-nilly.
Dazed, we pick a small bouquet of moments,
salvage our few futile remnants,
and grudgingly, tearfully remit our
squandered pension.

Heidi Hermanson has been published in *Backroads, Mental Horizons, Midwest Compilation, Slamma Lamma Ding Dong: An Anthology of Nebraska Slam Poets*, and other places. She has been in many public art projects such as "8 counts/24" (writers had 24 hours to write on a theme pulled from a bag) "OmaHome" (writers wrote inspired by a piece of artwork; the writing was then interpreted by a local actor), and the benchMarks project, which featured brief inspirational quotes on benches throughout the city. In 2003 she organized the first Poets' Chautauqua at the State Fair and also that year released her first chapbook, *Midwest Hotel*. Her second chapbook, *Missouri Joyride*, is forthcoming.

She runs a monthly open mike, "Naked Words." In her spare time she hopes to open a library of maps to towns that do not exist and learning dialects of the seven-year cicada. She recently received her MFA from the University of Nebraska.

City Erupting
by Ron Horner

kiss your fathers and your mothers
kiss your neighbors and your brothers
kiss your sisters and your sister's friends
take their hands
raise them high
600 miles long
this is our way
the Baltic Way
a human wall of paper dolls
One Million cut from the ticker tape
remember 1989

no lines
no lines drawn in sand or mountains or backyards
no red line
show your papers
I've got family on the other side
checkpoints
This is not how we will wait another 30 years
not cold in a war between allied nations
not against our crumbling hopes
and skies with the same sunrise
as our country men
we are the nation divided

governments put down their guns
and picked up propaganda
a diplomacy of appeasement
at the end of the second war
they never wanted a third
but this, here, is an iron curtain
and we are the palms of civil disobedience
through Dresden and Leipzig
through Hungary and Austria
we are the beginning

remember November 1989

the world is holding its breath
pressed against televisions and radios
I was 8 years old
third generation American
my grandparents still set the table
for cousins trapped inside Potsdam
crowding the living room
searching for swimming faces in the broadcast
Berlin is erupting

Wir sind das Volk
We are the people

Wir sind das Volk
We are the people

Wir sind das Volk
We are the people uniting

Das Bundesrepublik Deutschland
One nation
One people

Wer zue spaet kommt, den bestraft das Leben!
Life punishes those who delay
And we will wait no longer
We are the wall peckers
with our sledgehammers and our spirits
Here is where we were born
and here is where we want to live
walls can only keep people in
So join your mothers and your fathers
join your sisters and your brothers
and tear down
tear it down
tear down that wall

Ron is a two time member of the Omaha Poetry Slam Team and avid watcher of all things bad science fiction and fantasy. If you are lucky enough to find Ron in his natural habitat he'll be surrounded with source books, polyhedron dice, and trading cards. Don't Panic. Ron is a docile creature unless you threaten to take his pretzels.

Dark Rendering
by Jack Hubbell

She finds herself there,
damp stain upon cloth,
defined by an abrasive embrace.
A ward of the weave,
she turns inward,
    fold upon fold,
        ad   infinitum.
She of veiled entrails,
wound and Gordian bound.
Or so she would like to believe…

She in her soma of self deceive.
She in some wrecked   angle,
a tangle of falter alter-reality.
She an indelible Rorschach equation.
Forever a false façade in that there
with her goal of soul inversion,
the more she tried
   to collapse to center,
the more her core-evisceration
   rotated ever outward.

Spilling forth across a
gaunt canvas of hand drawn skin,
she had hoped to remain a
mute expanse of monotone grey,
and yet there from her pores
roared a riot of visual viscera.
She a painter's palette of
slaughtered pigmentation.
Her mind framed within that of another's.
A resolved composite of abject abstract
   emotive expression.
An ill literation of brush mental stroke
upon stroke

upon stroke
upon brutal relentless stroke.

And there she sits, naked and exposed.
Someone's delirium here transposed
with dark delusions decomposed.
Her mental mindscape scrolling forth
a perpetual reel of induced Hieronymus Bosch.
She, a Jackson Pollock jism skism of
both seared and sautéed psyche synapses.
She, a multitude of
mass maniacal machinations.
She, the same palette of chromatic hues
that in any other's harmonious hand
might resolve to render the
lithe petals of a lily's vibrant display,
yet by her own hand
    meld morose and
        magot malignant.

She with a slash of silver
painted across her throat.
She, gushing forth fountain the
deepest shade of pigment possible.
She, a vented pool
    of prismatic   perdition.
A kaleidoscopic cascade that
    bleeds and blends to black.

Extinguishing the candle.
Extinguishing the light.
Extinguished.
Ex-sting.
Ex-stun
Ex-pain.
Ex...   Extant.

She, rendered dark upon canvas.

She, now a portrait of death.

Primarily a visual artist utilizing photography and mixed media, Jack Hubbell has also held a lifetime romance with the art of poetic wordplay. A self taught writer, his involvement in the local poetry scene has seen his prose both published and heard upon stage at assorted open mic venues.

Jack hosts his own open mic event titled PROVOKE and this normally occurs on the first Thursday of every month.

Housing a Family II
Work in Progress
by David Prinz Hufford

I never could decide whether I should hide
my family in a cave, or let them take their chances
out on the open prairie with room to run.

I couldn't make up my mind if a castle would be better
than a cabin or a mansion or a tract house or a trailer,
the back of a car, a tent, the homeless shelter, or a dumpster.

Well, they got the tract house in the suburbs,
but for a time it was a trailer. They got an education
and never actually starved. They got the C+ American dream.

Whatever I did, it could have been better.
even this--in a spiritual sense--was still too much,
considering how Native Americans lived--or ancient Hebrews.

I mean, if you can't carry everything you own,
don't your have too much? Why would you envy
Anyone who has more than that?

Consider: Dante gave the envious souls in Hell
The pain of dragging through eternity everything they ever owned
While their eyes stayed sewn shut with wires of lead.

After all, on the short side of eternity
they could not see what everybody had
was more than they needed.

Well, now they don't have to look at it any more.
All they can feel is the endless drag of possessions
across a burning prairie.

David Hufford, sometimes called "The Professor," sometimes just Dave, has been writing poetry of record since age five, when his mother put his first poem in his baby book; and has been performing poetry since 6th grade when his teacher invited him to sing a song he had written. As a teenager he learned that girls were impressed if he sang a song he had written for them, and as a college student he learned that *some* teachers were impressed by the poetry he wrote. As a teacher of English language and literature he taught in five different high schools in two states and two countries, college in two states and three different countries, and has published many poems in several magazines and anthologies, three chapbooks of his own and given hundreds of readings over the past 35 years. An elderly gentleman, he still slams.

A Poem with Footnotes as read by A. Jameton
by Andrew Jameton

*This poem is called "Reminiscence." It's not by me, but was translated by a
scholar from the Cretacean language, one of the major language groups of the
late dinosaurs.*

*According to Wikipedia, the passage is based on tracings lifted by
paleontologists from much older sedimentary layers discovered while exposing the
fossilized footprints of early humans in South America (similar footprints have
been discovered near the Great Rift in Africa; in the African prints, two walk
together, one turns aside and then returns to the path). To preserve the delicate
patterns, the curator at the South American dig has had the area recovered with
vegetation and is working with district officials to establish the site as a
historical park:*

Reminiscence

I remember, it used to be as it was,
Sky red and quiet in the first light,
Horsetail and elephant grass squat and stately,
Stalks reflected trembling in the puddles.
The mud was always the best,
And roiling with friends in the cool dawn,
Squeaks and bellows; splash and thump.

Gerda her willowy neck weaving
Silhouetted against the sky
And her mottled belly stretched smooth by gumbo,
Her languid hips moiling about, always thinking
Of a better life for the Sauropod.
Stegs, Pachies and other trash down the way
Chewed noisily on ferns and snorted over salt,
Gossiping stupidly about the latest oviraptor scourge.

We Dip's and Pat's, we saw further.
We wove our patterns deep into the marshes,
Thinking of our eggs, the little ones to come,

Their tails flicker, sweet feathery fronds;
Their tiny legs one day to become the gnarly stumps
Of the Sauropod forest —
So long ago, before the sun dusted over.

It is unclear whether some of the extraordinary inaccuracies in this translation
are to be blamed on the poorly educated dinosaur poet or the distortions of the
anonymous scholar who translated the poem. The Cretaceous was the last great
age of dinosaurs. Horsetail (Equisetum) might have existed, but elephant grass
probably evolved later. Much dinosaur brain was located at the base of the
spine, and so strangely relocated thought. Sauropods is a classification of large
dinosaurs, including the Diplodocus ('Dip's') and Apatasaurus ('Pat's')
Stegosauruses you know from King Kong and Jurassic Park. Pachies
(Pachycephalosauruses) were noted for their thick skulls. Oviraptor ("egg
ravisher") fossils have been found so far only in Mongolia.

So long ago, before the sun dusted over.
Now the chill penetrates even my hide;
I wonder when the sky will clear;
The rain, when it comes, stings.
Our brittle soles and nails crack like mud.
We have roamed far from our ancestral bones,
Our children are scattered.

We'd best keep moving.
The land trembles less beyond the Gran Chaco, they say.
I can barely see, but it seems to me,
That the little crawlies who once vexed our step
Must now be hiding or dead.
It's been weeks since I have seen our cousins wing above.

We score our emblems intricate and deep in the soil;
We map the way for those who may come after us:
This ceaseless ache for mud fills our souls and moves us on.

The rain stings probably because it is acid after the great meteor crashed into,
perhaps, the Yucatan. The Gran Chaco is a great swampy plain in Bolivia,
Paraguay, and northern Argentina. The little crawlies are possibly mammals or

smaller dinosaurs, maybe roaches. The 'cousins' are probably the Pterosauruses, the flying reptiles.

We score our emblems intricate and deep in the soil;
We map the way for those who may come after us:
This ceaseless ache for mud fills our souls and moves us on.

[Culture and Entertainment] Gerda is likely named after the Winsor McKay cartoon Gertie the Dinosaur. The notion of dinosaurs making meaningful marks in the Earth is derived from the Calibans in C. J. Cherryh's, Forty Thousand in Gehenna (1983). The theme also echoes Langdon Smith's ballad Evolution, and Clarence Day's Scenes from the Mesozoic. And most powerfully, the Little Golden Book on dinosaurs by Jane Werner Watson.

Andrew Jameton is a philosopher on the faculty of the University of Nebraska Medical Center College of Public Health. He is on the board of City Sprouts, an urban community garden, and is working on philosophical issues in climate change.

The Jeweled Necklace of the Great Mother
Ishtar Hiding In A Pot of Gold
AKA
It's Red at the Top, but You're Never Gonna
Stop the Violets
AKA
Just Ask Roy G. Biv, Even He's Gonna Tell
You: Richard Of York Gave Battle In Vain
by Jarvis

He says the thing about rainbows
however alluring they may be is
they always follow acts of destruction
and the greater the act of destruction
the greater the rainbow

He reminisces
to a time when he was a child growing up in the Midwest
he bore witness to the storm of a century
he was knee high by the forth of July
and what lies before his eyes
is magnificently powerful
as his family's farm bowed before the sky,
and never stood back up
when all was said and done
the only reply
was a rainbow
great enough to calm the hearts
of the survivors

He said it was God's apology

I want to travel back in time
and view a rainbow from the bow of Noah's ark
in the after hours of the mabul hagadol

the greatest natural destruction in the world
I want to see the most spectacular rainbow ever sprawled out on
    the horizon

It was a million dollar rainbow, he remembers
and at least that much in damage to the farm - painfully repaid
but rainbows aren't underwritten into insurance policies
you're not gonna get 'em back
you're only gonna see them when they're farm fresh

The rainbow is the chaser
the storm is the shot
one of em's gonna push your wig back

Nobody ever mentioned how beautiful was the rainbow after Katrina
journalists never wrote of the sky's colorful frown - sorrow
like, we'll worry about tomorrow .... tomorrow
we seldom remember rainbow's like they're one of our own
see, if they named rainbows like they did storms
put the pictures on the wall to hang in halls of fame
we might be talking about them still
like with hurricane Andrew came rainbow Aretha
give a little respect

The greatest rainbow of my lifetime
rose above the destroyed wing of my grade-school in Kansas
and it was just as breathtaking as the tornado
they go hand-in-hand
a little good cop/bad cop
mixed with a little bit of David Copperfeild,
it's all just an illusion
Mother Nature's slight of hand

The rainbows we remember come after the storms that we forget
we set them aside from the chaos
as if they had nothing to do with it.
we never want to consider the rainbow
as a flag of victory

hung by the enemy army
as they laid claim to our own backyard

Jarvis is an Open Mic Junkie who represented Omaha on the 2009 Omaha Slam Team. He can often be seen at the monthly Omaha Slam and the Love's Jazz & Art Center Open Mic among other events around town. Jarvis can be reached at jarvistothe@gmail.com.

Eclipse
by Lydia Y. Kang, MD

Midday sun filters around a rock
Seamlessly slipping behind the smallness

Of stone that happened by chance
That day to be right there. We steal

Out of the buildings and wander
On lawns dappled with half moon flickers

Tiny crescent suns sift through stirring leaves
Caught on an outstretched palm under umbrellas of oaks

We look through smoky films lifted
Up to heavenly bodies that we were told never to look at

The umbra with its non-blinking eye stares back
And we continue to wander confusedly, lost

In the minutes of half-hearted darkness
And nearly living yellow-gold light

Lydia Y. Kang is a physician specializing in primary care internal medicine at UNMC. She enjoys writing poetry, creative non-fiction, and young adult fiction. Lydia has been an active member of the Seven Doctor's Project since the Fall of 2008 and her work has been published in *JAMA, Annals of Internal Medicine, CMAJ,* and the *Omaha World Herald.*

Cravings
by Liz Kay

In the grey hours of December,
I buy mangoes,
try to suck the shine from their flesh.

All winter I taste old death—dry
meat, raisins, hard
seeds. I crave the flavors

of the womb—wet fruit, young
calf, milk heavy
with cream, the warm flesh

of a fresh kill. From the bright swirl
of creation, we all
arrive, sticky as cut fruit. Little

wonder we slaughter the lamb each
spring, our throats dry
with the taste of the grave, hungry

to savor life at its beginning.

Liz Kay holds an MFA from the University of Nebraska, where she was the recipient of both an Academy of American Poets' Prize, and the Wendy Fort Memorial Prize. In 2008, she was awarded a Dorothy Sargent Rosenberg Prize for excellence in lyric poetry. Her work has appeared in, or is forthcoming from, such journals as: *Margie, Red Wheelbarrow, Whiskey Island Magazine,* and *The New York Quarterly.*

She was from Chechnya
by Brok "Tryst" Kerbrat

I woke up from the most terrifying dream
One so beautiful and heavy
So heart breaking and innocent
That it scared the hell out of me

I wanted to write it down
To see it grow in words
But I couldn't move from the couch
The tv blaring in the background
As I closed my eyes

She was a cheerleader
Green and gold emblazoned outfit
No pom poms or cheer squad
Just her
Standing tall amongst the lights
Holding up two fingers
A peace sign

She was from Chechnya
War still raging in her memory
I did not see her parents
Only her
Alone
Holding up two fingers
A peace sign

There are no cheerleaders in baseball
But she was there
Celebration and victory
The triumphant Little League team in the background
A small road to the side of the stadium
Where she was looking
For no reason than to make sure that if anyone was passing
She'd be the first thing they saw

This survivor and still-child
This celebration of youth and innocence
Holding up two fingers
A peace sign

No one mentioned the censorship
But it pulsed like road haze
Around her upraised hand
Pulling me into her defiance and exultation
Begging me to join her
To wash away the pixels
To scream at the camera
That you can not hide the sun
Holding up two fingers
A peace sign

I wanted to rush to the computer
To bring her to life
To see who she is
To give her a name
To figure out the meanings
To explain the dissonance
Because it hurt so much to keep it in
To not show her sweet existence
In a dreamscape so marred by broken mirrors
To believe that I can see hope
Holding up two fingers
A peace sign

I sat there
Listening to commercials
And the dim humming of the fan
Breathing heavy and slowly
Trying not to cry
Because my chest was not big enough
To hold her
Trying not to cry
Because I did not want to forget her

Holding up two fingers
A peace sign

Brok "Tryst" Kerbrat was once voted Sexiest Man of the Year by Better Homes & Garden. Unfortunately, the chaise lounge set of 2002 received many more votes. Abandoning his modeling career, Tryst took up writing. He accidentally started slamming in 2006, and since then has shared the stage with Johnmark Huscher, Mike McGee, Panama Soweto, that crazy drunk guy from the bar down the street, Rachel McKibbens, Robb Q. Telfer, and many more better qualified wordsters. He's been a member of two National Poetry Slam teams (2007, 2009), representing Lincoln, NE. "No Coast! What the @%$! is the ocean?!" When he's not planning further ways to burn furniture (grudges don't need upholstery), he's working on a poetry book and planning a tour in the somewhat never-too-far-away future. Look for him on your sidewalk, milk carton, or neighborhood post office. You'll recognize him by his worldly eyes and that scarf you "lost" at Target. "Live like you mean it."

I Just Knew Your Voice Was There
by Natasha Lianna Kessler

And I knew that the dead hen
Was laying eggs in the garden,
White eggs by the pond and wood fence.
We found one nestled between two brown eggs.
You told me how you wanted to steal my sugar cubes
And feed them to horses.
You didn't care to wear rain shoes in rain
Or fill the empty cat bowl.
You said one day you'd count my
Eyelashes to learn how many lives I'd lived.
I just knew the day would come
When you'd say you have to go
To the orchard
With a basket and a stone.
But the trees were bare.
You threw the stone to the sky
And with tears you pieced together a life.

Natasha Kessler is a graduate student in the University of Nebraska MFA program. She likes to dress her poodle in sweaters (it's cute) and fold paper airplanes at work. She co-edits the online poetry journal *Strange Machine*, www.strangemachine.com. *Strange Machine* accepts submissions year round from all levels of writers. Strange Up Your Life Today!

Poetry
by Bruce Koborg

Poetry,

Have you ever thought too much about things that most people take for granted?

Have you ever experienced a longing for someone who won't give you the time of day?

Do you find yourself ruminating over line breaks, rhythm, or the sounds of individual words?

Do you often wonder how you could invest hours of effort into writing something which few people will ever read, let alone get paid for your efforts?

Then poetry may be right for you.

Studies have found that poetry combined with a total lack of social skills and an aversion to all outdoor activities have let to ostracism, Marxism, feminism, shamanism, deconstructionism, syllogisms, verbal flatulism, exhibitionism, alcoholism, manic depression, self-obsession, onanism, anonynimity, excessive internal rhyming, madness, suicide, and, in extreme cases, even tenured faculty positions.

Discontinue use of poetry immediately if you find yourself excessively using words like, cicada,
soul,
death,
or revolution!

In some studies, poetry has been found to cause delusional
        thinking,
Symptoms can include:
Giving a contributor's copy or publisher's remainder as a gift

Imagining your tanka adapted into a TV pilot or screenplay.
Hours spent writing entire stanzas onto the back of overdue utility
    bills,
Increased facial hair,
Attempting to channel the ghost of Jack Kerouac via a coffee-
    stained Ouija board,
Excessive fear of cappuccino machines gurgling during the most
    heart rending line of a love poem for a dead classmate.
 In some cases after completing a draft, poetry has been known to
cause excessive wetness or an erection lasting for more than four
hours. If this occurs, immediately seek out your gender specific,
soul mate in the nearest coffee shop.

And remember to ask your writing professional about poetry.

Bruce Koborg has been writing poetry, off and on, for about 10
years. He has read at universities, art galleries, theatres, bonfire
parties, parks, coffee houses and bars. He is NOT fond of
removing Industrial Strength E6000 (medium viscosity, Clear, "The
Multi-Purpose Adhesive Self-Leveling Formula") from the
concrete wall at the Empty Room.
Contact info: brucekoborg@yahoo.com.

A Poem For Bree
by Greg Kosmicki

You want to know what love is
so I'll tell you what it is.
It's when I come out into the living room
and my daughter who is 18 years-old
is watching TV, and I say when
are you going to bed
because I can't write a poem
with you watching TV and she's
startled: *You can't write a poem*
if I have on the TV? See you
who do not have children who grew up
in the last twenty years or so don't know
that children nowdays think nothing of it
to listen to music, watch TV,
work on their laptops and read a book
or write a paper all at the same time
sometimes while eating a Hot Pocket
and texting someone on their cell phones.
So for me to not be able to do something
rudimentary as to write a poem,
rudimentary and antiquated and simple
as to write a poem, while a TV
is yammering away about Bea Arthur
and the Golden Girls and the breakthrough
for television that their show was,
while writing a poem—why wouldn't she
be startled?
How pathetic a creature I am.
She wanted me to get her a cookie
and I said *Ha ha not! Why don't you*
get me a beer and go to bed
so I can write a poem?
She said *You can't write a poem*
while the TV's on? and
got right up and I thanked her

and hugged her and told her
I'd write a poem about her
because she is so precious and full of love
that she gave up watching TV
just so her old man could write a poem
and she said I'll just go upstairs
and watch it on my laptop, so she
got a snack and went to bed, and I
went to the garage and got a beer
from the zillion cans left over
from my 60th birthday party
two weeks ago. Every time
I want a swallow of the beer
I've got to stop writing,
put down my pen,
pick up the can, put it to my lips
and tilt my head back—
ancient technology
passed down from generation
to generation, now almost outmoded.
Then I have to put down my beer can.
Then I have to pick up my pen again.
My daughter is upstairs in her tangle
of electronic devices like an astronaut
on the far edge of space
communicating with half the world at once
while I'm back down here, an ancient man
scratching along on a sheet of papyrus,
no, on a piece of stone
with a stick and some dim notion
that if I scratch long enough
 a word might break forth from the rock
where it had been locked up for us for ages.

Greg Kosmicki is a poet whose works have appeared in more than a hundred magazines, including *Poetry East, Cimarron Review, Paris Review, New Letters, Briarcliff Review, Pebble, Whole Notes, Connecticut Review, Sojourners,* and *New York Quarterly.* Greg has had 3 books and 6 chapbooks of poems published since 1998, the most recent of which is *Marigolds* from Black Star press in Lincoln.

Greg has won two fellowships from the Nebraska Arts Council for his poetry. He and his wife Debbie live in Omaha where they are both involved in social work. They are the parents of three mostly-grown children.

Imaginary Woman
by Henry Krusiewicz

My daughter's first razor was a gift—some
kind of pink-handled thing that
I picked up at Wal-Mart; she needed it
since other girls had begun making
fun of her—calling her caterpillar legs.

In my daughter's hand the razor scrapes
lather from tracks of new flesh; in its
wake blood beads well up from ankles
and backs of knees. My wife and I teach
her this art of taking away.

This first shaving is only the start: later
she will uplift breasts, line eyes, smear rouge
upon cheeks, darken lips. Such acts
will bring her pleasure; such acts
unfold in a simple fashion—
with an act of shaving that removes
her humanity one downy hair at a time.

Henry Krusiewicz lives and writes in the geographic center of the
United States: Fremont, Nebraska. He is married to wife Janice
Pemberton and has two glorious children, Konner 19 and Laura
16. He is an assistant professor of English and the Humanities at
Midland Lutheran College and is co-director of the Great Plains
Poetry Pile-Up.

At Dallas International Airport
by Mel Krutz

Cell phones, like clumpy jewelry,
dangle near ears of people sitting,
standing, walking, pacing all amongst
us, as if we are not there.
They do not care.

They laugh out loud, joke about,
chide, chortle, vociferously rant and rage,
argue, plead, repeat what they have said,
send love, shout, cry, spilling their souls
to the whole assembly at our gate.

We who wait, ears unadorned, cannot
think or talk amongst ourselves, or
concentrate to read or meditate.

Their resolute resounding voices
aggravate our space, pollute our
sensibilities, insult the air with
disconnected conversations.

They are like actors on a public stage,
and we, imposed upon with their
cacophony of skits in all directions,
cringe, but cannot defuse the
battering of sounds, the impinging
on our ears, the pounding in our heads
that this rudeness is.

Mel Krutz's poetry can be found in a variety of anthologies and periodicals, including *Plainsongs, Plainsong Review, A Journey to the Source of the Platte, Times of Sorrow / Times of Grace, Nebraska Life* and others. She lives on a farm near Seward with her husband Charles, where there are pleasant sounds of wind and rain, wild turkeys, cats, quiet deer, squirrels, rabbits, foxes, and other calm companions.

Dormancy
by Jen Lambert

In the spring, we travel north
and south over the country of our bodies,
wade through long tongued orchid
and wild iris spreading like white fire
at our feet. We eat olives, pine honey,
soft cheese while the cypress bend,
and watch our tongues explore.

In autumn we stay in, lock
the door between the cold
and us. The sweet gum blush
in the late sun, drop thin crimson
leaves at their feet. Our bodies are seeds
wrapped up to winter in the cellar.
Dormant in these conditions, we curl
shut like lockets.

Jen Lambert is an MFA student in poetry at the University of
Nebraska at Omaha. She is a part-time English instructor at
Metropolitan Community College and full-time mother of three.
Contact info: jencunningham@yahoo.com

Nebraska Annie
by Leo Marks

—After the linocut of the same name by Eddith Buis.

You see that girl
All done up
Ready to ride in the barrel race today;
You've seen her before
In the church choir, or
Lugging schoolbooks across campus
She's your neighbor
She's your friend,
And she only lives here, in Nebraska.

She's Nebraska Annie,
She puts the "good" in the Good Life;
All Nebraska's Annies
Make the great plains a paradise,
And the wide open prairie
Is the only home big enough for her heart.

She can change a tire
And make biscuits that melt in your mouth;
She looks perfect in her high heels as she climbs out of a pickup
        truck,
And in a state where the weather
Is always trying to kill you,
She's all the sunshine you need.

Nebraska Annie
Walks long and lean through the cornfields,
Lives in the sandhills and the streets and the railyards of our home,
She's the pride of the state in a state full of pride
And she loves like the secret streams of Nebraska,
Deep, and plenty, and clear.

When you're with her

You feel all the promise of the pioneers,
Unafraid and pushing toward the setting sun..
And her voice sounds like the wind in the buffalo grass,
And her voice sounds like the Platte stumbling over stones,
And her voice sounds like home.

Leo Marks is a guy you'll see at many local readings. His poetry is perhaps only bested by his shirt collection.

THE HUMAN COMMUNION OF SALT
by Clif Mason

Stars are tattooed on night's black skin
The moon shrivels like a leaf.
Neither mountains nor stars
are permanent—
just imponderably slow
in their infidelity to eternity.
Explosions in some other part
of the world peel skin
from our flesh here.
Glass slivers pierce our cheeks.
The graves of dead dreams
abrade our skin.
Pain takes apart everything,
even poetry.

A star begins to sing on my tongue.
If we wait to learn the words,
the song will be finished.
We sing without hesitancy or fear,
stepping blind off a cliffside,
knowing the path
will rise to meet our feet.

Every time I enter the daybreak meadow
of your presence,
I feel the shockwave and heat,
as if lightning has struck ten steps off,
ripping air apart,
stripping it of all but ozone.
You breathe air—pure as oxygen
fresh-minted in rain forest—
into my mouth
and invite me into the green chapel
of your love.
I walk into waking dream.

We kiss lips and bodies,
tasting cinnamon, taking
the human communion of salt.

Clif Mason is Chair of the English and Humanities areas at Bellevue University. His poems have been widely published in magazines and have won a number of awards. They have been collected in the chapbook *From the Dead Before*. Clif can be found on Facebook or reached at cmason09@cox.net.

The Baby is Very Busy This Morning
by Matt Mason

The baby is very busy this morning, she
hurries about the house picking up socks and books and
    microscopic dots and
rushes back to hand them to you

all the while, her face serious
as if she were deciding which wire on the detonator
to cut so that the dam doesn't blow.

You are not entirely awake; she
is motoring as if a coffee shop lives
inside her still-hardening skull, she

clearly has things to do, important things,
her "to do" list as long
as her arm,

well,
more so; reading:
chase the dog and jingle her tags;

check. Spill a small bowl of dry Cheerios across the floor;
check. Turn on the desk lamp with its cool circular switch;
check. Do it again;

check. And again;
check. Perfect this for several minutes;
check, check, check. Stop,

fart,
beam widely at this amazing accomplishment;
check. Unlock the secret of lever-style doorknobs;

not quite,
but it is only a matter of time as

she is so close;

and on and on, her nubby feet going
pat pat pat pat
across the kitchen floor,

circling you in your chair,
the black of every windowpane softening
to their inevitable, breaking light.

Matt Mason has won 2 Nebraska Book Awards; done poetry
programs for the United States Department of State in Minsk,
Belarus; and been published in over 150 magazines and
anthologies. His first full length collection was *Things We Don't
Know We Don't Know* (The Backwaters Press, 2006); look for it at
your local bookstore or online. Mason earned his MA in Creative
Writing from the University of California at Davis, then, of course,
moved to Omaha where he now lives with his wonderful wife
Sarah and baby daughters Sophia and Lucia.

He edits PoetryMenu.com, a listing of every Nebraska poetry
event; serves as Executive Director of the Nebraska Writers
Collective; and founded Morpo Press which, since 1997, has
published 30 chapbooks by up-and-coming local writers. Contact
him at mtmason@gmail.com.

Comfort Food
by Sarah McKinstry-Brown

I come from a long line of women
who insist on cooking up a religion
that is more starch than cumin,
calling on a God who measures
blessings. Most Sunday mornings,
I can be found on my couch,
watching cooking shows on TV,
searching for a God who is more Julia Child
than Charlton Heston, imagining a heaven
that is one big, small kitchen--a place
where all of our souls will eventually rise
to sit around the table and break bread.

I can see my grandfather
passing the butter to my grandmother,
while God putters around the kitchen
in her billowing white apron,
measuring and mixing flour, sugar, baking powder,
and when she spills a little salt,
pausing to throw some over her shoulder
to ward off the bad spirits.
And when a handful of the salt lands in the night sky,
she doesn't bother to sweep it up,
because she's not the cleaning type,
and she knows that all of us down here,
whose lives are messy,
more accident than precise recipe,
are hungry.

Sarah Mckinstry-Brown studied poetry at the University of New Mexico and the University of Sheffield, England and is currently earning her MFA. Her poems have been published everywhere from journals such as *The Harwood Review*, to Albuquerque's city buses, on Omaha's bus benches and West Virginia's Standardized tests. Most recently, she won the Blue Light Poetry Prize for her collection "When You Are Born." When she's not reading or teaching writing workshops across the Midwest, Sarah makes her home in Omaha NE, with her husband, Matt Mason and their daughters, Sophia and Lucia.

Sargent, Nebraska, 1982
by Kassandra Montag

It has not rained for weeks.
The once amaretto wheat fields
have dulled, their brittle
spines curved and hunching
over. The farmer walks
through them, listening to the crackling
and snapping, heel to toe.
Even the soil splits open in narrow yawns.
This is the only pleasure
he's had since Mary, the youngest
of his five, was born.
The sky runs on ahead,
chronic unraveling,
the only god he's ever known.
Her body is periwinkle
and soft, a fleece blanket
that wraps up the crippled trees
in the horizon, the bent fields,
and a lone house on a hill.
For years he has been tormented
by prayers.

Finally he decides it is far
enough. He stands nearly
in the middle of the field,
the tawny heads around him unmoving
even in the slight breeze.
The shot is heard by his wife,
three miles away.
That evening
their eldest son finds him
lying face up,
dry and colorless as the paper

wheat, his eyes open,
each a glass pitcher
the sky pours its blue into.

Kassandra Montag: I am a Masters student in creative writing at Creighton University, where I also work with arts administration. In May 2009 I graduated with a BA in philosophy from the University of Nebraska, Kearney, during which I self-published two chapbooks of poetry, had poetry published in the *Carillon*, and gave several poetry readings at the university and in the community. I live in Omaha and can be reached at kassandramontag@creighton.edu.

The Balance of Circles Choice
by Nabraska

Want that
which is just
unattainable; just
out of reach; just out
of view.
Call it envy;
And eat a lot of vegetables.
peas, broccoli, and beans.
Vision-
pathway to prosperity.
Light hits the pupil
and the iris turns green

Damaged dream, dream
deferred; R.E.M.
hits the retina
jarring consciousness awake.
Quiero Paz;
peace in my house,
peace with my city
peace with self.
knowledge, wisdom, understanding.
Re-know, Re-learn, Re-comprehend.
Know thy self
Be the cornea looking at
the reflection
as you cleanse
your lens
Light hits the pupil
and the iris turns green

Sankofa-
looking to the past,
solving problems of the present.
Brightness bends lenses

the pupils put to work
allowing certain shine in,
shuddering other illumination
Light hits the pupil
and the iris turns green

Eye of Horus
atop pyramids
as African heritage
is stolen
through the picking of cotton
on the backs of dollars,
like the backs of slaves.
Blinded by green backs
as Black backs are reddened
as an example-
You shall not turn a blind
eye to this, learn by sight,
even if the reflection
is upside-down
Light hits the pupil
and the iris turns green

Who is Nabraska? A poet, a teacher, an activist-some would say all
that and then some. He began his poetic journey as a youth, and
grew into his skills as a scribe through open mics, slams, features,
and performances, live, with musicians. Nabraska has toured
throughout the South, Midwest, West, and East coasts. He has
also taught spoken word workshops with youth through various
schools and community centers:
www.myspace.ccom/nabraskapoetryworld,
www.cdbaby.com/nabraska and remember every Tuesday
WORD on Tha Move: www.onthamoveradio.com.

Haiku
by Andrew "Bad Andy" Neely

I'm big in Japan but the grocery store clerk can't remember my
name

Johnmark Huscher, I'm
going to beat you until
the candy comes out.

We fight over oil,
but after we're gone, whose gas
tank will we end in?

I keep my feelings
for you warm... stuffed and mounted
over the fireplace.

You just can't feel bad
While you're holding a kitten,
Or getting a lap dance.

A tree falls in the
woods and no one is around.
Nature is a bitch.

People are driving
To work in 9 inches of snow
Damn, I miss the south

Andrew "Bad Andy" Neely was on the 2003 and 2004 Omaha
Poetry Slam Team and coached the 2006 team. He also made the
semi-finals in the 2004 PSI Head to Head Haiku Slam.

The Woman who Knows
by Charlene Neely

–inspired by the art piece Girlie Chair by Karen Thurlow

They wait with perfect posture
at the back of the chair,
everything neatly in place
handbags, hats and hair.

Except for the gray-haired one
who has learned her style fits her to a T
without all the accoutrements
demanded by the in-the-know society;

people in a city far away
who have the nerve to decree,
ridiculous or not this is the look
of the year for a proper lady.

And those who would brook the trend
and appear in public in anything less
must certainly be considered
to be a societal mess

This woman stands tall
knowing full well that all eyes,
including her companions, are on her;
for hatless or not she is confident and wise.

I want this chair.
No, I want to be that woman,
with the perfect gray hair and the courage
to know what not to wear.

Charlene Neely plays with words like a three-year-old plays with blocks -- shuffling them around, stacking up, knocking down and rearranging them until they suit her. She likes the sound, feel and look of words. She has lived in Lincoln and several small towns in Nebraska and Iowa.

Charlene is a member of Lincoln Chaparral Poets, Nebraska Chaparral Poets, Nebraska Writers Guild and several other smaller and more informal writing groups which all keep her muse on alert.

As half of the Poetry Ladies, we present programs in schools and other venues: http://www.freewebs.com/poetryladies/index.htm

Scarlet Bee Balm
by Molly O'Dell

Two hundred ninety five pound African-American female
Lived here all her life
A mountain cannot be moved
No primary doc, no follow up
Works four days a week
Needs pressure pills she got here last year
Out since Christmas
Mountain top removal's controversial
Didn't know she got sugar
Or eyes need special attention
I ask her the best part of her day
Wide as the underground mine
her gums shine like scarlet bee balm,
"Food, girl!"

Molly O'Dell practices medicine in Omaha, received her MFA
from University of Nebraska in 2008 and is a founding member of
the 7 Doctors project.

Resistance: Counting by Color
by Diona Poff

Mike gets a hard on when he scratches his head.
When he masturbates, his head itches.

He misses the girl whose identity you assume
when you're mostly absent. She's dead
but she won't stop crying and throwing leaves.

The left hand is tired of doing grunt work.
It breaks brushes and rips the canvas, makes threats
about a claw hammer and finishing nails.
Some of us are mostly fist and tears.

Mike can't reconcile his breath to his tongue
so his words come out all over his hands:
he's writing you poems to someone else again.

They're addresses of things he's lost.
He trusts you to find them, bring them back.

There's really nothing Diona wants you to know about her, unless
you care to ask.

Cobbler
by Zedeka Poindexter

I am a generation removed
from the Georgia, but I can't help loving
peaches like they sprang up in my back yard,
sang me to sleep at night.
They put me in the mind of mint juleps,
front porches,
summer dresses
How the rules are natural
as breathing, even when they are meant
to smother.

The rules are more important
Than the recipe; cobbler is about the texture
of things. How they stay close to the surface.

Sugar and butter
Not: oleo, Parkay, I Can't Believe
It's not BUTTER
Not: Splenda, Equal, packets of imitation
Sweetness; our reality
Lives in the little choices we make
To remain connected
To the food and the folk
Who taught us
What's important

Remember not just the cobbler's sweetness,
but the stories we tell; Over the years we lost
our accents, not our traditions

The flavor lies in the balance
Of cinnamon and nutmeg
The correct proportions
will remind you of your grandmother
Her slightly red complexion

in summer; her hand cupping
under the spoon as she offers
you a sample of what she learned
sitting on her mother's floor
listening to her hum.

> *The key is in the buttery citrus that remains*
> *on your tongue ; senses are memory-*
> *used properly they transport you home*

Zedeka Poindexter is a published poet who has also competed for
poetry slam teams from Omaha and Colorado Springs at the
National Poetry Slam.

Eutanasia
by Prahduct

He said he wanted to die And what's strange is his lips never
professed these things But I could see defeat written all over his
face He wanted to surrender life Have his soul snatched from his
body Cause that flesh and those limbs were 3x5 cells to his spirit
His feet barely touched the ground 'Cause something inside of him
wanted to levitate Toward the skies His heart beat outside of his
chest 'Cause it being inside of him wasn't enough to keep him alive
He said the most alive he ever felt was in his sleep And wouldn't
mind living there for eternity And he told me all of this and didn't
even speak I read it in between each open and close of every blink
There are death notes written on the inside of his eyelids And he
rewrites them each night in his dreams Praying to die as he looks
on the outside at folks dying to live Saying to himself that could
never be me And he's got me wishing I could Travel through
history And meet the day living felt like dying And tell hope to
come faster than a heartbeat And tell death it can't live here, not
for a minute longer But how do you convince someone life is sweet
When every spoonful of life got their face all wrinkled up wishing
for a glass of death to wash the taste from their tongue the
acquired taste of life scraped clean from the plate the sight of the
leftovers scraped is enough to bring tears to his face cause the after
taste of life is still fresh on his mind tastes like blame that's been
sitting out for the longest time and I'm waiting for the moment to
slip in the line "it's not your fault" but that statement has rang in
his head for years now and has had no luck in getting through so
what am I to do, what is he to do? When that flesh and those limbs
feel like 3x5 cells to his spirit His feet can barely touch the ground
Cause something inside of him wants to levitate Toward the skies
When His heart beats outside of his chest Cause it being inside of
him isn't enough to keep him alive Prisoner to his own guard Steel
bars of shame gripped within his palms Nothing left to do but to
die Somebody in the cell next door Morse code to him… life Tap
freedom on the floor Many of he are amongst we Those who can't
remember to forget Become those we forget to remember The
walking dead Our sister, brother, mother, father, friend Needing

to be welcomed home again And reminded of the sweet taste of life.....

The relationship of art and life are forever intertwined to create the product of experience. Whether broken into the genre of creative writing, painting, sculpting or performance poetry, Omaha native and artist Shukura Zuwena Huggins finds a way to incorporate her art as a reflection of life. As a poet, Shukura was given the name "Prahduct" which has proven to be a true testament of her encounters with several talented artists, which have influenced her life and ultimately her art. The name Prahduct is simply a reminder that everything she's doing is not because of who she is, but rather because she is a product of those who've come before her and are here right now. Prahduct began seriously writing her thoughts and ideas in the form of poetry, prose, and song during her freshmen year in high school in 2002. Her always-present love for creative writing began to transform into a love for performing what was written which was sparked by several different experiences with poets near and far. Continually acting as a student of the art of spoken word, Prahduct continues to improve her skills and truly deliver a unique style to performance poetry and the spoken word movement.

Make Star Sex, Not Star Trek
by Todd Robinson

–for Matt Mason

Just let me sit
like Lieutenant Uhura,
stalwart and dusky
and you won't be sure
if you can hail the enemy ship
       until I find the frequency
          every time, baby,
cuz I ain't no strange new world,
I ain't no new civilization.

Let me love you like Kirk:
I may be impulsive,
but I can whip
Romulans into submission
as I have phasered
countless villains into subatomic
particles that shine and shimmer
like the ultradiamond ring
I will slide on your green finger,
like the collars we wore on Triskelion,
you, enthroned,
kohl-eyed next to some ersatz Caesar
as I dive and roll in the arena, shirt in tatters, shouting
       "without freedom of choice
    there is no creativity.
      The body dies;
  Leave bigotry
   in your quarters;
there's no room
  for it on the bridge;
 no more blah! blah!
  blah!
 Worlds are conquered,

galaxies destroyed…
but a woman is always a woman."

Let me love you
like Bones,
with a love
than can heal you of anything;
    let me love you like Sulu,
    in the most velvety voice this side of Deneb;
        let me love you loyally, like Scotty;
            let me love you without the need for six or seven increasingly
                                    lame movies to milk us for
                                    the money we won't even use
        in the 24th century, sci-fi socialists
spiraling through space,
    let me love you
    without equals or sequels or abominable prequels,
        let me love you like a Klingon,
            swarthy and swaggering and "Heghlu'Meh QaQ
                            jajvam!"

beautiful,
let me love you boldly,
and I will love you
        logically:
    like Spock;
because I want to mind-meld
with you, baby;
    after a time, you may find
    that having is not so pleasing
    a thing, after all, as wanting.
    It is not logical, but it is often true;
it is the *ponn farr* -
the time of mating.

Todd Robinson miseducates the youth in the Writer's Workshop at UNO, serves on the board of the Backwaters Press, and has been an avid participant in the Seven Doctors Project. He has been published hither and thither and has several fancy degrees.

This is A Journey into
by Ru-Sel

It stands the tests of time from the lips and papyrus
strips, scripted and shredded between the very beginnings of
human expression. It co-exists with nature interchanging with laws
of man, land and the laws of love. Carved stone upon stone buried
and carried on bumble bee wings prickly hair-like whispers taking
the shape of clay to be molded with the living souls and once
breathed but no more. It has wrapped and defined our everyday
happenings like the finest of silks from the far east, hand sewn and
pigment died to blend and transcend through all fabrics, textures,
textiles, surfaces, ethnicities and cultures. It descriptively grows
lush low in the valleys between stoic snow capped statues, giving
nourishment but always feeding more than our bellies, our bodies
our total self. It can pierce you hollow without breaking the skin
and ease you with out touching you, meeting you, knowing you...it
knows. It can be the left-overs of a sleeping loved one or the smell
of a fresh babies neck. It is that one piece of furniture that
completes your living room set. It is the hat she wears, the bracelet
always on her left wrist, the song in her head. It is his first car, his
high school diploma, his first haircut he paid for himself, that flush
that rush. It has a pulse, vigorous and sounding of thunder yet
owns no pair of shoes you or I could fill alone. It is the meaning of
money, the reasoning in love, it morphs into the taste of the world
telling shapes like braille raised and goose bumpy....like sign
language to the birds that take our thoughts in a message to rain
upon soldiers, children, the down trodden, the forgotten, in strange
lands and unpredictable circumstances. It is the brightest light at
the end of a long rusted tunnel, the groves and soot at your
footsteps amplifying that crackly gritty sound each step you take
counting your breath nervously staring forward but reflexes are on
a cloud, anticipating anything-Anything.... It's the sour stomach
when your first dream has died, that creamy cold scoop of
ice-cream licked once then plummets to the ground like a rock. It is
the fruit on the trees with it's rotten core, it's the decimal pebbled
sands each significant grain from shore to shore. It has the power
of lightning striking with the tickle tickle of an ostrich feather....

It is never the end of an era
It is always made new
It can never be read incorrectly because it displays and represents
      too many faces to fault just one
It is your waking thought at dawn and your last on the eve of your
      life
It can be viewed from the stars and bubble forth from the darkest
      seas
It is everything in and between you and I
It is every character in every language, tongue, dialect dictating and
      directing our existence, beyond our futures
It is imprinted on our dna strands and encased within us forever!!!

It Is Poetry
It Is Poetry......................in motion

Though the prose and cons subjugate the weight and the balance,
my style of stanzas overstand and out measure conventionality.
While most of my peers consider me a prolific writer, my
poetry/writings tend to be very abstract. My starlit journey will
potentially result in various, all inclusive books of poetry.
–Ru-Sel.......The Painter

You Can't Say *I*
by Marjorie Saiser

Resist much.
—Walt Whitman

Imagine the authorities telling us we can't say *I*.
Imagine the fines I'll have to pay:
500 for *I will*, 500 for *I want*, 500
for *Do I*?

And then the next decree
comes down: no *my*, no *mine*.
You, *my* friend, friend of *mine*,
may have a stash of *my* and *mine*,
jingling around like quarters

but authority can clip a hole in the pocket of your blue jeans
with sharp silver scissors. You still have a *Could I* and a *Should I*
in one pair of shoes,
hidden under the arch supports.
Walk around on that.

There have always been people telling us you can't say *I*.
What do they say, *I* wonder, to their mirrors in the morning
or when they sit in their meetings?

There have always been people like us, common as grass,
who stand with the best posture they can muster
and sometimes hold hands or link arms
and walk down the road
hearing a certain beat in the body,
one foot saying *I*, the other saying *we*.

Marjorie Saiser, named Distinguished Artist in Poetry in 2009 by the Nebraska Arts Council, has work at http://thebackwaterspress.com and at www.poetmarge.com.

Once Past Pluto
by Bud Shaw

When you left me to go to
space,
we were underwater and
I was drowning in steel and light and blood.

You must have swept 'cross Moon's dark
seas
looked back and
saw me stumble.
Did you laugh or whisper,
let go?

On Mars, you could pilfer dust and through your glass take
Phobos'
soul
while I scrubbed knuckles for the sake of pride and
wished you couldn't wince
when I push.

You were always in range, of
course.
But when you answered,
from Titan or Phoebe or Europa's icy plain,
we longed for resentments and
cherished your secrets.

Back here all seems so
serious,
their analysis mundane,
their beards long,
their mothers loathed.

While they total your troubles and foretell your
stay,
I go looking for you in my regrets and

find you floating across to Neptune
hoping for revenge.

In the living room, on the couch, across the dog from the
fireplace,
I watch you pass Pluto in an incandescent bulb and

escape sparks again.
I didn't know I was still here.
We were fine growing dear and
spare.
I could do that for as long as it took waiting
for closure and
that flicker.

And then she was here and
though late
she told me about the pebbles he stuffed in her mouth and
the taste of stone,
about rope and wire
around her wrists and
I heard my pulse

again.
You were gone so long, always far
away
and even when you turned back you
didn't and too late and—
And I left.

Bud Shaw: I am a frustrated writer who fell into a bad crowd and
eventually ended up a becoming a former transplant surgeon and
former departmental head. I write fiction and creative non-fiction.
This was my first attempt as an adult at poetry.

DANCE
by Michael Skau

The late night radio news was pretty depressing;
even the sports was mostly scandals: steroid use,
illegal gambling, and rape investigations.
The cabin seemed thick and close with gloom,
so God and I went out for a walk. Some birds,
I don't know what kind, were creeing high in the breezy
night; the moon, three-quarters full, shone
like an egg, surrounded by shell shards
in a star-rich sky. Down below, moths were chasing
the light from where I hadn't pulled the curtains
tight, and were chased in turn by something dark
and swift, perhaps a bat? Crickets
squeaked as we stood in wonder. Then God began
swaying rhythmically back and forth,
and the birds and the wind and the moon and the stars
and the moths and the bat and the crickets and I
paused to watch God dance to music I couldn't hear
under the trembling aspen leaves.

Michael Skau is a Professor of English at the University of
Nebraska at Omaha. His poems have appeared in *Carolina Quarterly,*
Northwest Review, Paintbrush, Kansas Quarterly, Laurel Review, Passaic
Review, South Carolina Review, Sequoia, Texas Review, and *Blue Unicorn,*
among many others.

Options
by Meredith Smith

At November dusk, the gray sky cracks
like a nut, and blue stripes wriggle
snakelike between clouds and leafless trees.
The city bus lurches between stops,
all engine mutter and hissing brakes.

The white dots on her red dress are prim
as Pilgrims, clustered in soundless threes,
abiding the hard plastic seat. Even
this time of year, her legs stick. It's Tuesday.
She ponders supper choices in biblical extremes:
Lean Cuisine (the righteous)
or leftover cannelloni (the damned).
The window keeps gray twilight
a cold weight against her shoulder.

They are at her stop. She stands, legs smacking
free of the seat, descends
the steps. And on the last step-
she stops. In front of her is
an option.

The option is wearing a gorilla-suit glove.
All she can see is an arm,
a hand, dangled over the roof of the bus.
It bars her way. The hand has an offer:
a white paper shopping bag
filled with red, red apples. It swings slightly.

She stops, peers upward, sees nothing
of face or identity. Steps to one side,
to go around. The bag shifts,
blocks her way.

Trapped on a bus

by a bag of apples.
Fancy that! A dilemma.
She loves dilemmas.
Should she grasp the bag?
Should she bolt past, scattering apples on the curb
like shrunken heads?
Should she grab the gorilla-arm and pull,
fling the gloved man from atop the bus?

"Lady, get on or get off."
The bus driver is impatient.
He cannot see the apples. She nods,
turns back to the apples, still unsure.

The bag is white as a bonnet, the apples
red as stop signs. The gorilla arm is patient.
She looks past it. Beyond,
she can see her house, her walk,
  the bright spots of her chrysanthemums.

"Lady, NOW." The driver taps his fingers
angrily against the wheel.

Yes, now! She takes a step,
ready to push past-then
grabs the plastic handles,
like Eve or Betty Crocker.
The force of her decision shakes
the sky and knocks the house windows crooked.
She whirls as the bus pulls away-
there is no one on the roof. She considers the bag,
then turns, to go eat cannelloni
and bake a pie.

Meredith Smith is a graduate of the University of Nebraska's MFA in Writing program. She teaches writing part-time at the Buena Vista University center in Fort Dodge, Iowa, and works full-time in theatrical costuming (making smashing hats, shuffling papers, and occasionally dressing as a carrot). When not writing or masquerading as a vegetable, she enjoys reading Dr. Seuss over and over again to her daughter Lyra, gardening, and doing mosaic glasswork.

MIDNIGHT SHADOWS
by Phil Smith

Insomniac's fate
To brood so late.
Nocturnal gloom
Where shadows loom
Rhythms deep
of family sleep
can't push the dread
out from my bed.
So I get up and piss
Into Kafka's abyss

Phil Smith: I am an infectious diseases specialist at UNMC. In the past I had written poetry intermittently, but none recently, until Steve Langan invited me to participate in the Seven Doctors Project. Thus inspired, I began writing again. Poetry serves as a cathartic outlet for the powerful emotions that the physician's role engenders.

Dig
by Sam Stecher

Sometimes I think I want to be a superhero
because I get tired of seeing zeros in people's eyes
like they were robbed of the sight of hope
like they are living the nightly news every day
living what was the TV dinner glow broadcast in high definition
      from that side of the world to your house
from that coast to your home
from that side of town to your TV glow
from that side of the street to your window in real life picture
      almost as good as a
high definition broadcast
There seems to be a lot of death in high def
like we were all living in a vacuum with a void that could only be
      filled with blood and blame
like all we had to do was blame the people that were the rot
drill them out and pack them back in the cavities as filling

It makes me want to be a superhero
because I could hide some bodies
if I could hide the bodies of the people making people into
      nobodies
If I could dig the graves of a few
before they kept the gravediggers of thousands in steady business
I think I could I do that
But I'd rather be superhero with power of a gravedigger in reverse
Because I get tired of blame

Blame is a logic more flawed than love
the former is more often placed and later is better shared

So I choose the superpower of a grave digger in reverse
Rather than hide the bodies those blamed I will dig up the graves
      of the people we needed back and give them life
I got shovels for angel's wings and I got shovels in spades
and I'm not digging holes I'm digging them out

I'm not digging graves I'm taking them back

like David Halberstam so he can tell us about when baseball was a
    game and not a science experiment
dig
like Evel Knievel so we can get money spent hell bent and I want
    to trade him this poem for a motorcycle and have everyone
    follow me over the cars and the canyons
dig
like the King because we need to tell him we are still dreaming
dig
like the other King because we need a little less conversation and
    some more showmanship
dig
like my dog Cruiser if for no other reason than I miss him dig
like Joe Stecher because we need to fight like the heavyweight
    greatest with unlimited rounds best two of three falls so we
    can fight though our mistakes with disregard for what
    round we might go down in
dig
like Kurt Vonnegut because we can't write anything as big as
    glaciers or as big as war or the powers that stop them but I
    need to somebody to tell me to keep trying
dig
like all four of my great grandmas the two I never met, the one
    never knew when she wasn't crazy and the one that gave
    me hugs like she couldn't break so I can ask them was it
    you that put this in me
dig
like Jimi Hendrix because we work to do in mountains and the
    edge of a hand isn't enough we need axes to cut this shit
    down
dig
and Cormac McCarthy
and I know he isn't dead yet but he's not a young man and he
    needs to be on the list because some day I might need to
    ask him where is this road

And I know this won't work
I'm no superhero
Shovels don't bring people back and they don't give flight to angles
        no matter what you say your wings are made of
But they can do so much more when you're not just trying to
hide the bodies of the blamed

So pick up a shovel unfold your wings
and dig

Sam Stecher engages in educational pursuits and poetic follies from
his home base in Kearney, Nebraska supported by his lovely wife
and numerous large dogs. He also goes by Olaf Graybeard,
Charter Member of The Neo-Norsemen of the Pedal Stomp
Revolution.

Excerpt from Prologue, *Mermaid on the Prairie*
by Maureen Tobin

I had a bookcafe in Iowa, in an old brick building on the corner of Alfred and Main. This was three blocks from the intersection where Highway 173 (known in town as Main Street) crosses Highway 44 and becomes M66 (also known as Bluebird Avenue.) Your map may not have Kimballton on it, so it will help to know that it lies napping in the triangle formed by Harlan, Atlantic, and Audubon; each of these towns is thirteen to eighteen minutes away, in daylight and good weather. To orient you further, Kimballton is located in Audubon County, ten miles north of Interstate 80 and about halfway between Omaha and Des Moines, a little closer to New York than to Los Angeles.

The land between Kimballton and her neighbors was mostly planted to corn and soybeans. There still remained, at the time of my story, a few small farms, evidenced in the fields, terraces, windbreaks, and tree-lined creeks, in the undulating rows and irregularities that I'm told would not be tolerated on a modern corporate farm. Evidence also in the pungent, earthy smell that greeted the traveler passing an enclosure holding ten, twenty-five, maybe fifty or a hundred head of cows or pigs or chickens, maybe a few goats or horses, animals fed by someone who ate breakfast at the kitchen table in a nearby house.

Odds were good that when he finished his chores, he drove to a job, as did his wife. It was hard in those days for a small farmer to get by just on farming. (It may be still, or maybe the world has wised up, found a way to respect this hard work. Or maybe in the time you are reading this, the small farmer is an antique, a legend, and everyone eats food from factories. From where I sit, the future is up for grabs.) There were far fewer farms than fifty years before, or twenty-five years, though the acres under cultivation measured pretty much the same. Some farmers told me so much hard work was good for marriages, that farming required a partnership. The solitary man or woman might be overwhelmed by it, though there were some that did it anyway.

Maureen H. Tobin teaches high school English in Omaha and is a graduate of the University of Nebraska's MFA in writing program. The Seven Doctors Project has been a gift to her writing. She is also proud to be affiliated with the Graphite Sky Writers and the Poetry Warriors.

Gertrude
by Michelle Troxclair

My grandmother used to grease my scalp and braid my hair
And though sometimes painful, I didn't care
The stories she'd tell intrigued me so
How her mother was murdered by a white man
And left by the side of the road.
At 6 years-old, with her new dark-skinned mother
Chastised by a white man for not holdin' open his door
And how, when she was 12 or 13
The KKK marched down her street
Throwing stones and bottles, lookin' for niggas to beat
One of those stones caught my grandmother square in the crown
    of her head
Tears I shed,
As I used to grease her scalp and braid her hair
That 2 ½ inch scar still there.
She'd tell of her journey north to find work
How she cleaned white folks houses, took in laundry and ironed
    their shirts
How she cut bacon in freezing cold and the meat-packin plant
Til she scarcely had feelin' in either hand.
I'd rub them with Ben-Gay, along with her legs
With gnarled hands how she'd clean chitterlings, greens & make
    deviled eggs
My grandmother used to grease my scalp and braid my hair
And though sometimes painful, I didn't care
The stories she told and lessons she shared
Showed me there is nothing I cannot bear…

Michelle Troxclair runs poetry events at the Loves Jazz and Arts Center. She started their Poetry in Motion series.

Poetry in Motion, a monthly Spoken Word event, was brought about by a need to continue and to perpetuate an African American tradition that encompasses the creative manipulation of language and dramatization to tell stories, pass on history, relate experiences and report pertinent news. It has since morphed into a platform by which local writers and performers can hone their talents and promote their works.

All artist/poets are welcome. LJAC does not believe in slams or passing judgment on the works of those who bravely bless the mic. Join LJAC every third Thursday of the month at 6:30p.m. Food and beverages served.

Fathers
by Miles Waggener

In the terraced room whose floors are stairs
                between two
doors room enough for them they have
                come for us as if
attracted by our talk of them how they
                shielded us
from what we are unprepared to see shield us
                more they want to
endanger us take us along before headlights
                mountain roads
where more pictures will be taken take us
                to the man who
looks to be sleeping merely posing as what
                they wait in
the poorly-lit-in-between dressed for pictures
                children keep they are
confused trying to keep what they kept
                together and left
leave us they have come to fail a little more to
                wait for us to come
home to interrogate the time to rend the hour
                from us they know
we cannot sleep as if toward a coughing child
                they step inside with
water without knocking through thin walls many
                rooms they hear us

Miles Waggener teaches creative writing at UNO, where he
coordinates The Missouri Valley Reading Series. He lives in
Omaha with the writer Megan Gannon and their new son Manny.
This poem was first published in *The Antioch Review*.

Epistle for the Great Blue Whale
by Rex Walton

Just imagine what it's like to live in the under-world:
your body the size of a 747 fuselage;
your heart the weight of a Lexus;
your tongue that would tip the scales
above the tonnage of an average Indian elephant;
your flanks the sheen and shimmer of a mossy boulder
on the edge of a cliff on one of Colorado's 14,000 foot peaks.

Your brain: so ancient, that war
is a figment, or only a minor plot
in one of your tone poems;
or how you sing long,
spiraling stories
of your thousand-year culture
you tell to your young,
which they store completely,
and pass on, if they survive, to the future.

For the Blue Whale, the depths of the ocean
are an easy task, anytime:
the tail a luxuriant frippery of grace and force,
augering that body through this water-world
that hangs as solid and uncompromising
as a mantle on this earth;
as a shroud on this rock;
as a baptism of liquid fire;
as the anointing by some celestial priest of passage,
of communion complete and constant;
as the liquid sprinkling of the final rite;
as death enters the mirror of the waters, as death
lumbers up
on the tip of a sailing ship, ready.

Think of the explosive head of a modern killing harpoon:
a surface -to-surface short-range missile

against a people who only wish for
tiny krill: an impossibly small creature
who passes into this earth, passes into the whale,
tons and millions at a time.

Think of our krill: the tiny populace of an Asian village;
the containment pens of South African apartheid;
the walled-off penitentiary of the Palestinian settlements of Israel,
the survivors in the refugee camps of Darfur. The wavery,
haunted streets of East LA, the continual depression zones
of the South Side, Chicago. The poor proud people living in
Nebraska's poorest counties: among the poorest of this nation.

We swoop, swallowing the name of a god, in the name of a
security,
in the name of Commerce, Justice, Order. The Corporation of Us.

We spit out nothing: we swill, swelter,
burn, and digest: how is this
a rite of passage to civility, or honor?
How can it be anything
but shame we cover with a thinning veil
of forgetfulness, of scandal
enveloping all.

Think of our children, waiting, watching, growing: what
do they learn when the harpoon
arrows the deep blue side of a Great Blue Whale?
What do they learn from
our fractured forgiveness,
our consummate forgetting,
our constancy of delusion, our
temple of the eternal self?

The blue whale, largest, eats only the smallest,
flies the ocean as a culture and civilization whose peaceful mantra
must be at odds with our own: why do we continually take their
    bodies,

pulverize them, hammer them, winch them
into the holds of a floating vivisection machine;
peel the great blue body
into long strips
we feed to the heat,
the fire,
the pulverizing?

We are at war: a killing, exterminating war,
with the People of the Deep --

yet we consider ourselves civilized, forbearing, calm, ethereal.

The English language has over a million words in it, and
continuing:

can we not take in this mass, each of us, opening our heart
to this swimming deluge of opportunity and conjecture?
Can we not, at the same time, bend our hearts to
peace, for the children of our world
as well as theirs?

Can we not begin to learn, newly, wholly:
a singing, a chant
to mourn our prior passage through these waters,
a keening dirge for the opportunities lost,
then, perhaps, a next verse of
hopefulness?

So, let the tune meander,
mourn, surge, celebrate: fight for
some reckoning, some better direction.
Take in a lesson from the Great Blue Whale:
teach our children a different wellness,
teach our selves to defend the brothers of this earth, not
eat them slowly, out of a great blue bowl; the hand
automatic, repetitive, digging, grasping more,
the eyes looking into the uncomprehending

stare of ourselves, coming back from the window,
our continual nighttime leaning closely to the glass,
the next day far off, and waiting with expectancy
for a change in our dream.

Are we not civilized men?

Rex Walton has been writing poetry for nearly twenty-five years,
beginning in the mid 80s as a student of UNL English professors
Greg Kuzma, Marcia Southwick, Mordecai Marcus and Warren
Fine. He co-edited the English Department's *LAURUS*
undergraduate annual magazine with Season Harper, and has
infrequently sent off packets of poems to publications, and has
(infrequently) seen some of those poems in print, such as *Plainsong*,
and the *Plains Song Review*. A poem of his was used as the lyrics for
Color of Silence, a musical piece by Anthony Lanman
(http://www.thenewstyle.org/catalogue.php?id=54). For five
years, he ran the Crescent Moon Reading Series at Crescent Moon
coffee in Lincoln, and worked with the NE Summer Writers
conference for three years, setting up the evening readings at
Crescent Moon.

Reflections
by Felicia Webster (AKA: Withlove, Felicia)

sometimes
in the movement of life
we meet people
we connect with on a soul level...
they intersect our current lifestyle with hints of sunshine
and rainbows
like they've known us from before
across time and space
our epic memory reminding us
of a once upon a time
we

we are everything
everything so so real
it almost seems too good to be true
but the equation balances
distributing every feeling
like electricity
zapping us to live in the moment
tantalizing us to have more emotions
then sneaking up into our thoughts at odd moments
replaying like a favorite John Coltrane melody
jazzy
and
snazzy
each note vibrating in tenor sax
like a fluttering heart beat
increasing adrenalin
and rapid breathing

inhaling energy
exhaling the world's pressures
we feel at home
together
but
in doubt
or fear of what's real
we stop to question it
over analyzing the time
asking
how could someone so new to our lives
exhibit so many qualities
we've only said we desired in our hearts and minds?

yet we
forget
life
moves
without prompting at times
slow ing us d
o
w
n
just enough
to let us know that it listens to our desires
on a soul level
and the happiness we feel with those we have connected with
exists in us
and they
they
just come along
in our journey

to remind us of the beauty, love and realness of it,
as our reflections.

Felicia is a long-time organizer and force on the Omaha and
Philadelphia poetry scenes.

Stung
by Ben Wenzl

I hope you don't get the wrong impression of me.
It's just that I've never been good at public s-...
with public sp-...public spppELLLLLLLLLLLLLing.

The shit went down at the Elementary school spelling bee.
I was in the sixth grade; it was the year 2001.

"We'd Made It Through the Wilderness!
We'd Made It Through the W-"...Y2k,
and if I had survived the enormity of the Y2k bug,
surely I could handle a little ol' spelling bee.

A-E-I-O-U

Y?

Because we like you!

...Or do we?

I'd never been the "it" kid, but I could spell the word "silhouette"
backwards so fast it'd make you question the way you brought
up your children.

And then it happened.
I had qualified for the school spelling bee!
This was the first athletic
(OKAY, THEY SHOW THAT SHIT ON ESPN)
event to which I was considered superior.
And you better believe that my unknowingly gay self
with the freshly flossed braces and the double-buttoned up collar
and the comb over hair and the lucky Mickey Mouse watch from
Burger King

were ready to ROCK THIS SHIT.

And suddenly the spotlight is on me, and with bated breath I stand
and await the word that Fate will send my way...

Gingerbread

GINGERBREAD! Oh, the sweet taste of having
the easiest word in the entire bee!
I rhetorically regurgitated my spelling shtick:

Definition, please?
Language of origin, please?
Use in a sentence, please?
Are there any alternate pronunciations?
Am I pronouncing the word correctly?
Gin-ger-brea-duh? GIN-GER-BREA-DUH?!?!?!?!?

I was ready.

Gingerbread.

G-I-G-E-R-B-R-E-A-D.

And I sat back down, all smarmy and smug.
And my teacher just stood there, mouth agape going,
"Ugggggggggggggg...I'm sorry, honey, but that's incorrect."

...

WHAT THE FUCK WAS THAT BITCH TALKIN'
       'BOUT?!?!?!?!?!?!?
Of course I spelled it right!
The easiest word!
My tongue and teeth created harmonious beauty
and had never been wrong before.

...Until the day that *FUCKING* "N"
was forgotteN from GiNgerbread, goddamNit.
I ran from the stage, crying hot

blue ribbons into my mother's boobies.

And come every December, the Ghost of Christmas Past
comes a'hauntin'. And I can smell the putrid scent of defeat
as I walk past every bakery in town.
Spell and spell as well as you can,
you can't spell me, I'm the *GIGERBREAD* MAN!

A-E-I-O-U?

And sometimes, we don't ask:

y?

Ben Wenzl, 20, semi-collegiate, um...loves coffee.

Organism was more than just a one-month poetry series: it was a product of many different styles, communities, and ideas of what poetry and art can be.

It brought together events through the help of The Backwaters Press, the Omaha Healing Arts Poetry Slam, the Nebraska Writers Collective, the No Coast Poetry Slam, the Seven Doctors Project, PoetryMenu.com, furniture artists Peter Cales and Doug Kiser, even bringing in visual artists, musicians, and yoga (Yogatry, baby!).

The Backwaters Press
(www.thebackwaterspress.com)

The Backwaters Press was founded by Greg Kosmicki in 1998, a non-profit 501-(C)-3 corporation, which has published more than 60 books, with a concentration on poetry. Books from the press have won numerous awards from the Nebraska Center for the Book, with Aaron Anstett's collection, *No Accident*, winning the Backwaters Prize, The Nebraska Book Award for Poetry, the Balcones Award from Austin Community College for the best book of poems in the country that year from a small press, as well as being a finalist for the Colorado Book Award.

The Omaha Healing Arts Poetry Slam
(www.omahaslam.com)

The Omaha Healing Arts Poetry Slam happens at 7:30pm on the 2nd Saturday of every month at 1216 Howard Street in the Old Market. Founded in 2002, it has gained an impressive reputation nationwide, known for great writers gifted with great performance skills.

The Nebraska Writers Collective

The Nebraska Writers Collective is a non-profit organization dedicated to putting poets into schools as teaching artists and also to put on great events featuring talented local and touring poets in Nebraska communities. Matt Mason is the new Executive Director, send him questions at director@newriters.org and send tax deductible donations to 9712 N 34th St, Omaha NE 68112.

The No Coast Poetry Slam
(www.myspace.com/nocoastwriters)

The No Coast Poetry Slam happens at Meadowlark Coffee & Espresso (16th and South Streets, Lincoln) at 7pm on the 2nd Thursday of every month.

The Seven Doctors Project

Physicians based at the University of Nebraska Medical Center joined Omaha writers during spring 2008 to collaborate on the Seven Doctors Project. I encouraged these seven doctors to begin, sustain, or return to projects in creative writing (or the writing of music, in one case). I was inspired by Dr. Molly O'Dell's presence as a poetry student in the University of Nebraska MFA in Writing program, where I teach, and by my friendship with the late Dr. David Dolan. Prof. Andrew Jameton, UNMC philosopher and ethicist, helped me conceive the project. The UNMC Institutional Review Board gave us the green light. Seven local writers helped lead the debut group, which met for eight weeks. The writers provided encouragement, mentorship, and their keen editorial eyes to the doctors...who began to work in earnest on their poems, stories, essays and songs...and presented them, despite their admitted nervousness or maybe because of it, to the group for feedback.

We made an early decision to help each other craft *publishable* work. Which means we frequently told one another the current draft isn't good enough...and provided suggestions for revision. One conversation led to another, and sometimes the dialogue led to revelations of one kind or another. Doctors don't get that opportunity often enough. We paused a few times to acknowledge the various therapeutic effects of doing creative work as a community of learners. The writers took the lead; the seven doctors became apprentices, a role not entirely comfortable for many of them. Through our group interactions and my pre- and post-interviews of the research subjects-and while shadowing them at work, an opportunity I really enjoyed-I was able to learn about their work up close.

Beyond any of our doubts, we became a genuine community. Several of our members are publishing. Others are right on the cusp. The fourth phase of Seven Doctors Project (or "7DP"), which currently includes more than 20 doctors and 20 writers, concluded on November 12, 2009, at the Empty Room. Ten members of our cohort read that night. It was a special night. On behalf of 7DP, we thank Matt Mason and his collaborators for assembling this anthology and including our work in it.

PoetryMenu.com

PoetryMenu.com lists every poetry reading in the state of Nebraska, from open mics to book festivals, poetry slams to featured readings. For information or to sign up for the weekly emailing of events (which goes out to over 200 emails), contact poetrymenu@novia.net.

Peter Cales

Co-creating ORGANISM at the Empty Room was an amazing, challenging, and ultimately, very fulfilling project. I had never done anything that approached an installation before, and came out with a new understanding of the collaboration, time commitment and work necessary to pull something like this off. I entered the project apprehensive of how the various components would work together; after all, there's not much of an immediate connection between poetry and building. But after some initial trial and error, we reached a happy medium. In the end, I don't think it was so much a collaboration as it was an exercise in sharing. Matt hosted several successful poetry readings and slams in the early part of each week. Doug and I took advantage of whatever chunks of time (mostly weekends) we could to build the Organic Chair and recreate a venue in the space.

For me, the most valuable part of the experience was having an opportunity to work with Doug. I already had a great amount of respect for Doug as a person before collaborating on the Empty Room project. But working with him allowed me to learn new design and fabrication processes and grow as a designer and builder. So, I came out of the project with even more respect for him and his work, and with an energy to put toward new projects.

I had the good fortune of getting to participate in two of the six Empty Room projects, and both experiences - while very different - allowed me to work in creative ways without worrying about money or an end product. It was very liberating, and a testament to the creative potential and opportunity available in Omaha.

To learn more about the work we did at the Empty Room, or my work in general, visit www.share-a-chair.com or www.measurecutcut.com.

Doug Kiser

Doug Kiser has written a few good poems and has constructed a couple nice things. His songs are pretty good and he's sold a bunch of paintings too. Someone said nice things about one of his sculptures in a newspaper. Come to think of it, that's happened more than once. He's been given awards for his work, nationally and internationally, and has been published or written about in numerous rags throughout the country.

Doug operates as d KISER design.construct, inc. remodeling kitchens, bathrooms and small spaces and making custom furniture. More information is available at www.dkiser.com.

Poetry / Organism

	Local Wonders Nights	Backwaters Press Nights	Poetry Slam Nights			
	Mon	Tue	Wed	Thu	Fri	Sat
1 3-5pm Grand Opening: Day of the Dead Poets	**2** 7-8:30pm Todd Robinson, Jack Hubbell, Heidi Hermanson, Prahdurt, and Marissa Gill	**3** 7-8:30pm Michael Skau, Jennifer Lambert, Rex Walton, and more	**4** 7-10pm Shout! Group Poems w/ Katie F.-S and Sara Lihz, Andrew Ek, Marissa Gill, Jarvis, Pat McEvoy, Zedaka, Sam Stecher, music by the Korey Anderson Trio and Little Black Stereo	**5**	**6**	**7** 2-3pm Matt Mason and Sarah McKinstry-Brown poetry reading
8	**9** 7-8:30pm Michelle Troxdair, Dave Hufford, God's Gift, Miles Waggener, and Steven Evans	**10** 7-8:30pm Greg Kosmicki, Lorraine Duggin, Liz Kay, and Michael Catherwood	**11** 7-8:30pm Haiku Slam and the Lincoln Poetry Slam team, run by Bad Andy	**12** 7-8:30pm, the 7 Doctors Project reading	**13**	**14** 6pm, Yogatry w/ Megan Minturn and Katie F.-S. Explore yoga, poetry, and music. Suggested donation: $20. Register at emptyroomyogatry@gmail.com
15	**16** 7-8:30pm Nebraska Diona Poff, Dominique Garay, and Henry Krusiewicz	**17** 7-8:30pm Marjorie Saiser, Shelly Clark, Molly O'Dell, and Cat Dixon	**18** 7-8:30pm Sock Puppet Slam (2 rounds, 8 competitors) and Omaha Poetry Slam Team	**19**	**20** Look Again: Artists and Writers. information: prairie.sky@gmail.com	**21** 4:30-6pm Local Wonders w/ Felicia, Bruce Koborg, Deirdre Evans, Susan Aizenberg, Kassandra Montag, and Lauren Goldstein
22	**23** 7-8:30pm Sam Stecher, Leo Marks, Devel Crisp, JV Brummels, and Neil Harrison	**24** 7-8:30pm Clif Mason, Mel Kurtz, Carrie Helmberger, and Gary Dop	**25**	**26**	**27**	**28** Closing Ceremonies
29	**30**					

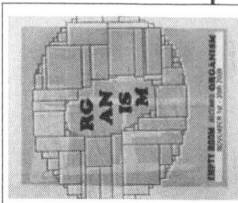

Organism

At The Empty Room: 720 N 13th Street (North side of the 22 Floor apartment building at 13th and Webster, sort of behind FilmStreams) You are invited to bring poems to hang on the walls. The walls start empty on 11/1 and will be papered with poetry by the 28th!

More details at PoetryMenu.com/emptyroom.html

All events: suggested donation $2-$10 to pay artists and cover costs. Extra goes to non-profits.

Brought to you by Matt Mason, Peter Cales, Doug Kiser, The Nebraska Writers Collective, The Empty Room, What-Cheer, Secret Penguin, and Poetrymenu.com